Moving is Relating

ACKNOWLEDGEMENTS

Thank you to all the teachers who evaluated and / or tested these lessons:
Gary Burdge, Anna Flynn, Daniel Johnson, Claudia Krase, Alina Rossano.

Thank you to the fourth and fifth grade students
at Orca School for sharing their lesson on emotions with me.

Thank you to Daniel Johnson and Gail Gustafson
for sharing their expertise in Laban Movement Analysis.

Thank you to Anne Green Gilbert, the Creative Dance Center faculty
and the participants in the 1997 Creative Dance Center Summer Institute for Teachers
for their ideas, feedback and inspiration.

Thank you to Thomas Christopher for his skillful photography,
and to my Creative/Modern students and their parents.

Thank you to Marisa Smith, Eric Kraus and Julia Hill
for their help and support in creating this book.

DEDICATION

This book is dedicated to Daniel Johnson for teaching me about moving, and about relating.

Published by Smith and Kraus, Inc.
PO Box 127, Lyme, NH 03768
Copyright ©1998 by Helen Landalf
Manufactured in the United States of America
Cover and Text Design by Julia Hill
Photographs © Thomas Christopher

First Edition: February 1998
10 9 8 7 6 5 4 3 2 1

The Library of Congress Cataloging-In-Publication Data
Landalf, Helen.
Moving is relating: developing interpersonal skills through movement, grades 3–6 / by Helen Landalf. — 1st ed.
p. cm. —(Young actors series) Includes bibliographical references (p.).
ISBN 1-57525-123-X
1. Movement education—Psychological aspects. 2. Dance—Study and teaching (Elementary)—Psychological
aspects. 3. Interpersonal relations—Study and teaching (Elementary)—Psychological aspects. I. Title. II. Series:
Young actor series.
GV452.L35   1998
372.86'044—dc21   98-9253
CIP

Moving is *Relating*

Developing Interpersonal Skills through Movement Grades 3–6

Helen Landalf

YOUNG ACTORS SERIES

A Smith and Kraus Book

Contents

Introductory Material

Introduction 1

Chapter One
Moving is Relating
Beyond the 3 R's: Why Teach Interpersonal
   Skills? 2
The Intrapersonal and Interpersonal
   Intelligences. 3
Relating Is Moving…Moving Is Relating 4
Experience, Reflect, Apply 5

Chapter Two
What are Movement Concepts?
Movement Concepts Chart 6
A Partial Listing of Locomotor and
   Nonlocomotor Movements 7
What Are Movement Concepts? 8
   Body 8

Space 9
Quality 12

Chapter Three
Basic Effort Actions
What Are Basic Effort Actions? 15
Table of Basic Effort Actions 16

Chapter Four
How to Use this Book
When To Use the *Moving Is Relating* Lessons In
   Your Classroom 17
Preparing Your Students For Movement-Based
   Lessons 17
Using the *Moving Is Relating* Lessons 19

Chapter Five
Managing Movement 23

The *Moving is Relating* Lessons

PART I
INTRAPERSONAL AWARENESS 27

Section A: Identity 28
Lesson 1: Movement Signature 28

Section B: Emotions 31
Lesson 2: Identifying Emotions 31
Lesson 3: Changing Emotions. 33
Lesson 4: Emotion Garden. 35

Section C: The Self in Action 37
Lesson 5: Spontaneity and Control. 37
Lesson 6: Acting with Power 39
Lesson 7: Risk and Commitment. 41

PART II
DEVELOPING INTERPERSONAL
SKILLS 43

**Section D: Maintaining Personal
Boundaries** 44
Lesson 8: Personal Space. 44
Lesson 9: Personal Space Conversations 46
Lesson 10: Keeping Your Own Rhythm 48

Section E: Valuing Diversity 50
Lesson 11: Diverse Choices 50

Section F: Objectivity 52
Lesson 12: Interpretations 52

Section G: Communication 55

Lesson 13: Mixed Messages *55*

Lesson 14: Listening *57*

Lesson 15: Asking Questions *59*

Section H: Interdependence 61

Lesson 16: Independence–Interdependence . . *61*

Lesson 17: Changing Relationships *63*

Lesson 18: Making an Impact *66*

Section I: Trust 67

Lesson 19: Empathy *68*

Lesson 20: Consistency *70*

Section J: Cooperation 71

Lesson 21: Movement Machine *72*

Lesson 22: Compromise *74*

Lesson 23: Collaboration *76*

Section K: Leadership 78

Lesson 24: Leading and Sharing Leadership *78*

Lesson 25: Changing Leadership *80*

Appendices

Discography 82

Bibliography 84

Sample Creative Dance Lessons

Lesson 1: Place *86*

Lesson 2: Relationship *88*

Introduction

For the past ten years I have had the privilege of teaching Creative Dance to children in a variety of settings. I have taught afterschool classes in private studios for children of upper-middle class parents. I have taught weekly classes for very young children in preschools. I have worked with groups of up to thirty elementary and middle school students in large urban public schools, as well as classes of five in tiny rural schoolhouses. I have taught classes for gifted children, for children with special needs and everything in between.

It has always been exciting and gratifying for me to witness the creative and technical development of my students — to see children who have never danced before expressing themselves through their own choreography, to see a toddler hop on one foot for the very first time, to see the unbridled enthusiasm of a fifth grade boy (who initially thought dance was "for girls") as he leaps boldly into the air.

It soon became apparent to me, however, that something beyond creativity and skill was being developed as children danced together. I noticed that the children in my creative dance classes, whether they were preschoolers or sixth graders, began to treat their peers with an unusual level of thoughtfulness, understanding and respect. They were careful not to make an unkind comment; careful to make sure that everyone's ideas received consideration. The level of bondedness among the children in these groups was noticeable to anyone who walked into a class.

The amount of interpersonal growth that was being spontaneously developed as a result of children moving together was brought home to me one day in an afterschool class of eight, nine and ten year olds. Many of these children had been dancing together in my classes since age three. One girl in the class, who was a newcomer to the group, was a rather difficult child. She was often whiny, bossy and argumentative. One afternoon as I was dividing the students into groups to work on choreography, I overheard Amanda, a new but popular student, say to Josh "I hope she's not in my group." His reply was "We don't say things like that in *our* class."

Anyone who teaches children between the ages of eight and ten will attest to the fact that Josh's concern for the feelings of his unpopular classmate and his sense of allegiance to the values of the class is quite unusual. Yet I realized that I had come to expect this type of mature, empathetic behavior from children.

I'd also like to tell the story of David, a fifth-grade boy in a public school in a low-income neighborhood in Montana. I had been warned by David's teacher, and by the school principal, that David was a "tough guy" and would probably cause trouble. As it turned out, David was intrigued by dance and was a highly creative mover. Near the end of my week-long residency, when it came time for the fifth-graders to choreograph their own dances, David's interest was intense. He actually asked me if I would keep the classroom open at lunchtime so his group could practice!

The dance that David's group choreographed, and which they performed for the entire school, was a dance about fighting. While I initially balked at the choice of theme, I soon realized that doing a "fighting dance" was a wonderful way for David to express his pent-up feelings. The resulting piece of choreography was stunningly graceful, and so carefully executed that only the gentlest possible touches were used. The principal thanked me for helping David find a way to express himself and commented that, during the week of my residency, David had not engaged in a single playground altercation — usually a daily occurrence.

The incidences of bonding, empathy and self-expression among the children who danced with me were taking place as if by magic, without any conscious effort on my part toward making them happen. As I myself became more aware of what was taking place I began to experiment with directing my students' awareness toward the interpersonal aspects of a dance lesson instead of just hoping that the magic would continue. The resulting experiences and discussions led me to believe that what I was doing was valuable for children and that I should be sharing it with other teachers.

The lessons in this book are the results of my experiments and experiences with teaching children about self-awareness and interpersonal relationships through movement. I hope you will enjoy moving, relating and reflecting with your students as much as I have with mine. I leave you with one warning: come to these lessons with an open mind. Never believe that your students are "too young" to understand and discuss these topics. You are in for some amazingly perceptive insights, and some profoundly moving experiences.

Chapter One
Moving is Relating

BEYOND THE 3 R'S: WHY TEACH INTERPERSONAL SKILLS?

With her very first cry a newborn baby signals her innate urge to communicate with others outside herself. From infancy, human beings are driven to interact with others in order to meet basic needs and to develop a sense of self. Even in the first months of life infants are capable of complex human interactions. By the time they are one year old children are able to communicate needs, wants and emotions to their primary adult caregivers, and can receive communications of anger, worry and love from those same adults. Our urge to relate is strongly connected to our will to survive.

Although we come into the world equipped with a natural inclination to relate, traditional societies have always taken care to train youth in the interpersonal skills required in the culture into which they were born through direct instruction by elders and through rites of initiation. Early European society trained its young people into their societal roles and appropriate behaviors through instruction in complex codes of customs and manners. Even American society had its finishing schools and debutante balls for the purpose of developing the ability of young people to relate to others and to fit into the predominant culture.

Times have changed, however. No longer are gender roles and society's behavioral expectations as clear cut as they once were. The options for appropriate lifestyle, career and relationship choices have expanded to a degree that might have been incomprehensible even fifty years ago. No longer is there a single, agreed-upon code of behavior and values in our culture.

This is all to the good. The new openness in our society provides a means for individuals to choose the lives, relationships and ways of being that are most truly expressive of themselves. However, we may have thrown out the baby with the bathwater. Not only is there no longer one dogmatic set of mores for young people to follow; there is also very little guidance available at all in how to understand themselves, how to interact with others and how to make the decisions that will impact their lives.

I recently spoke with a friend of mine who has an eleven-year-old daughter. Her daughter is capable in academic subjects, but is miserable in school because she does not have the tools to form relationships with her peers. "Schools teach children all the other subjects," complained this parent, "but they expect children to know how to make friends."

Reading, writing and arithmetic have long been thought of as the three fundamental "R's" that students need to be taught in order to function in our society. I would also like to propose a fourth R: relating.

THE INTRAPERSONAL AND INTERPERSONAL INTELLIGENCES

The mother I spoke of in the previous section was obviously aware of the emphasis in our public school systems on what educational theorist Howard Gardner calls the logical/mathematical and verbal/linguistic intelligences. Gardner has postulated that these are only two of the seven or more intelligences which human beings posses. Among the intelligences that he describes are two others around which the lessons in this book revolve: the intrapersonal and interpersonal intelligences.

The intrapersonal intelligence is the intelligence that regulates self-knowledge, including a sense of identity and awareness of how one is feeling and behaving. Many popular self-help books and seminars have the purpose of guiding adults in developing their intrapersonal intelligence.

The interpersonal intelligence deals with the ability of a person to relate to others. The ability to form relationships, to communicate effectively and to be a good leader are all functions of the interpersonal intelligence.

Obviously, these two intelligences are related. Without some degree of self-knowledge it becomes nearly impossible to relate to others. And how else do we learn about ourselves but through the perception of those around us?

The intrapersonal and interpersonal intelligences are also linked with the ability to function effectively in all of the other intelligences. Take the eleven-year-old mentioned earlier, for example. Although she is naturally competent in her academic subjects (probably utilizing the logical/mathematical and verbal/linguistic intelligences) her lack of skill in the interpersonal area makes her unhappy and negatively impacts her concentration, self-esteem and motivation — all of which are necessary if she is to work at her highest potential academically.

To give another example that many classroom teachers are familiar with, imagine that a child in your classroom has parents who are currently going through a divorce. The child, however, has very little awareness of what he is feeling about the situation and very little ability to express his emotions. No matter how brilliant a lesson you present in math, language arts or any other subject, this child will probably be unable to receive the instruction you give due to his sense of intrapersonal turmoil.

As a matter of fact, some students called "field sensitive" students will most likely be unable to receive any information at all if intrapersonal or interpersonal disturbances are present. These students, according to Herman Wittkin, are those who take in the whole picture before they are able to see the details. They are often especially sensitive to the emotional climate of a learning situation.

Not only field-sensitive students, but all students are highly impacted by their relationships to peers, teachers and family members. In spite of this fact, interpersonal experiences tend to be minimized in today's classrooms, where learning is often individualistic and competitive. Students are trained in the idea that they need only focus on their own goals; that they will be seen as more successful if their peers are less successful. Interpersonal skills decline further as classroom computer use accelerates, and the interaction between student and computer becomes more prevalent than the relationships between students and their classmates. This focus on the individual deprives children of the experience of commitment to a greater community.

The negative impact of a lack of focus on the intrapersonal and interpersonal intelligences should by now be apparent. The benefits of providing students with guidance in these crucial areas are numerous. A primary benefit of addressing the intrapersonal intelligence in the classroom is student self-awareness. Students who are aware of their own strengths and weaknesses are better equipped to manage their own learning and assume responsibility for their choices.

Mastery of interpersonal skills will be invaluable to young people not only in learning situations, but in their future careers and personal lives. Such mastery leads to a greater ability to work cooperatively with others both in the classroom and on the job, to form and maintain relationships of all types, and to provide leadership in any group or community. By providing direct instruction in the intrapersonal and interpersonal realms a teacher is not only making a sound investment in the emotional climate of his or her classroom, but in the future lives of her students.

RELATING IS MOVING… MOVING IS RELATING

If they are addressed directly at all, interpersonal skills are most often approached through listening, reading, writing or discussion — in other words, through the verbal/linguistic intelligence. The lessons in this book, however, utilize a combination of the verbal/linguistic and kinesthetic intelligences to address these skills. Why is the kinesthetic intelligence — learning through physical sensation and movement — an important instructional tool in the interpersonal area?

In the area of relationships and communication, so much takes place outside the realm of language. From the very beginning of life an infant has feelings and makes interpersonal connections, and only later is able to distinguish those feelings and label them with words. Even as adults most of us have had the experience of being unable, in words, to express what we feel or to adequately describe our relationships.

Much of our interaction with the world and the people in it actually takes place in movement. The movement may be as obvious as physically drawing away from someone we distrust, or as subtle as a change of facial expression as we listen to the communication of a friend. Similarly, we naturally observe the movements of others in order to discern what they may be thinking, feeling or trying to communicate. Because we are so attuned to the movement inherent in relating to others, movement becomes a perfect vehicle for examining those relationships.

Not only is movement inherent in relating — relating is also inherent in moving. Every movement of the body causes a change in physical relationship: The body may change its relationship to itself, as when an arm is lifted above the head. The body may change its relationship to space, as when a person walks to a different place in a room. The body may change its relationship to an object, as when a person who has been sitting in a chair stands up. Or the body may create a relationship to another body, as when two people embrace. Thus, the relationships which are created as a natural part of human movement become metaphors for relationship to oneself and to others. Experiencing such a metaphor in physical movement can provide students with a deeply felt "aha" experience, which then becomes a springboard for reflection on the relationships in their lives.

In a movement-based lesson the whole child is engaged — body, intellect and emotion or spirit. Insights gained in movement are highly likely to be retained, as physical movement is regulated by the cerebellum — the part of the brain which stores muscle memory, and which facilitates the mind in grasping and remembering abstract ideas. Using movement to explore interpersonal skills generates learning that is both deeply impactful and long-lasting.

EXPERIENCE, REFLECT, APPLY

The model used in the lessons in this book is one in which students *experience* an insight through movement, they *reflect* on what they have experienced through class discussion or journaling and they *apply* the insight to their daily lives. In this way intrapersonal and interpersonal awareness is developed in the controlled context of a movement activity, then is crystallized through discussion or writing so that it can be later applied in the unpredictable context of actual human interactions.

It is impossible to move through the world without relating; without touching the lives of others. My wish is that we nurture a generation of students who know "in their bones" the meaning of communication, empathy, trust and leadership, and are responsible not only to themselves but connected and committed to the others who make up their world.

MOVEMENT CONCEPTS

BODY

Body Parts:	Head, Arms, Elbows, Hands, Back, Stomach, Legs, Feet, etc.
Body Shape:	Straight, Curved, Angular, Twisted, Wide, Narrow
Balance:	On Balance, Off Balance

SPACE

Place:	Self Space, General Space
Level:	High, Middle, Low
Direction:	Forward, Backward, Right, Left, Up, Down
Pathway:	Straight, Curved, Zig-zag
Size:	Big, Medium, Little
Relationship:	Over, Under, Around, Through, Together, Apart, etc.

QUALITY

Speed:	Slow, Medium, Fast
Rhythm:	Pulse, Breath, Pattern
Weight:	Strong, Light
Energy:	Smooth, Sharp
Flow:	Free, Bound
Focus:	Single focus, Multi-focus

A PARTIAL LISTING OF LOCOMOTOR AND NON-LOCOMOTOR MOVEMENTS

Locomotor (traveling)	Non-Locomotor (stationary)	
crawl	bend	squirm
gallop	carve	stretch
hop	dab	swing
jump	flick	turn
leap	float	twist
roll	glide	wriggle
run	poke	wring
scoot	press	
skip	punch	
slide	shake	
slither	slash	
walk	spin	

Using this chart

The words on this chart may be called out as suggestions during any portion of a lesson in which students are moving freely. For example: if students are exploring moving with different emotions in Lesson 3: Changing Emotions, in addition to cueing them with the Movement Concepts on the preceding page ("What Speed will you use to express sadness? What Body Parts might express joy?") you can invite them to incorporate various locomotor and non-locomotor movements into their exploration. ("How might you jump if you were suspicious? What would a surprised turn look like?") Being reminded of these words as they explore will help students vary the kinds of movements they choose to do instead of always walking or running.

It is highly recommended that you make a large copy of both this chart and the Movement Concepts chart to display whenever you are doing a movement activity so that you can refer to them easily while teaching. Your students will also find it helpful to refer to the charts when creating and evaluating choreography.

Chapter Two
What are Movement Concepts?

The basic movement concepts discussed in this book were originally defined and recorded by Rudolph von Laban in the 1930's in his attempt to describe and analyze movement and to establish a notation system for movement similar to the one used to notate music. These concepts underlie all movements, whether they be dance steps, athletic feats, pedestrian movements or even the movements of animals or machines.

Over the years many variations of Laban's vocabulary have evolved and many movement educators, myself included, no longer adhere strictly to his original terminology. In this book I use vocabulary similar to that developed by Anne Green Gilbert, an internationally recognized dance educator and founder of the Creative Dance Center in Seattle, Washington. Though my organization of the concepts is slightly different from Gilbert's, it is similar enough to make this book compatible with her highly recommended materials (see Bibliography). For the purposes of this book I have divided the concepts into the following three areas:

Body: including the Parts of the body that can move and the Shapes that the body can take.

Space: where the body moves in space, including the Level, Direction, Pathway and Size of a movement.

Quality: whether the movement is slow or fast, strong or light, smooth or sharp, etc.

The following section contains a short description of each Movement Concept followed by a simple idea for exploring the concept with students in the upper elementary grades, with particular emphasis on the role the concept plays in intrapersonal and/or interpersonal awareness. You may want to read this entire chapter once to acquaint yourself with all of the concepts. It is also suggested that you refresh your memory by reviewing the related concept(s) before teaching one of the lessons in this book. This will facilitate your ability to present the lesson clearly to your students. For a complete listing of the concepts see the Movement Concepts chart preceding this chapter.

BODY

All of the concepts in the area of Body define how the body itself moves exclusive of the body's relationship to space, time or other people. Since the body will be the instrument for learning and self-expression in the following lessons this area of movement will always be at play, even if not referred to directly. For pre-adolescents, who are dealing with a changing sense of their physical selves, the Body is an essential concept to explore.

Body Parts:
Head, Neck, Shoulders, Spine, Arms, Elbows, Hands, Stomach, Hips, Legs, Feet, etc.

The body can be divided into many different parts which can be moved in isolation (i.e.: standing still while only moving your head), in combination (i.e.: moving elbows and knees simultaneously) or moving all parts together as one unit. Body parts can lead us through space, move us along the floor and help us create shapes. Depending on their personality and cultural background, different people tend to emphasize particular body parts as they move. For example, a person who is often hurried may walk with her head jutting forward. Another person may make large gestures of his arms while speaking.

Idea for Exploring: Have students stand in one place. Call out the name of a body part (i.e.: "elbows"). When music plays, students will move only that part. When the music stops, they stop their movement and listen for the next body part to be called. End the exploration by asking students to move a body part they tend to move often, and then a body part they tend to move very seldom.

Shapes:
Straight, Curved, Angular, Twisted, Wide, Narrow, Symmetrical, Asymmetrical

Our bodies can make shapes. If we stretch all of our body parts a straight shape is created. When we bend our joints we are making an angular shape. Softening or rotating our body parts creates shapes that are curved or twisted. Shapes can also be wide, narrow, symmetrical (the same on both sides) or asymmetrical (different on each side).

Shapes can remain stationary, like a still photograph in one spot, or they can move through space. It is also possible for us to change shapes while we are moving. We can make shapes alone or with other dancers.

Idea for Exploring: Divide students into pairs with one student being a sculptor and the other student a lump of clay. The sculptor molds the clay into a shape, then copies that shape. Reverse roles. You may ask sculptors to make one of the specific types of shapes listed above, or encourage them to create their own. Emphasize the gentleness and empathy required when touching another person.

Balance:
On, Off

When our body is on balance, as when we're standing with two feet planted firmly on the floor, we feel stable and connected to the ground. When our body is off balance, as when we lean or tip, we feel as if we might fall. The challenge is to go off balance, but still be in control.

We can make many kinds of balancing shapes: balancing on one foot, on a hand and a foot, on a bottom, etc. We can also go off balance as we move by tipping, swirling or spinning on one leg. Some students will enjoy the dizzying feeling of being off balance while others will prefer the security of being on balance.

Idea for Exploring: Encourage students to experiment with the many types of balancing shapes they can create. Call out specific body parts for them to place on the floor (i.e.: "Balance on one foot…two hands and one foot…your stomach…your back"). Next, challenge them to create balancing shapes with a partner, perhaps even carefully balancing body parts on each other. For example, one student might make a middle level (crouching) balancing shape while a partner balances his or her leg on the first student's back.

SPACE

The concept area of Space defines the expanse we are moving through and how we get from one place to another. The same principles of Space apply whether we are moving in a large gymnasium or in a small corner of a classroom. The more students understand about their relationship to space, the more orderly and less confusing the physical world will seem to them.

Place:

Self Space, General Space

The concept of Place tells us whether we're moving on one spot (Self Space) or traveling through space (General Space). Movement done in place is called non-locomotor movement while traveling steps are known as locomotor movements. (See listing of Locomotor and Non-locomotor Movements preceding this chapter.) Whether we travel or stay in one place, we each have a personal space or kinesphere which serves as a boundary between our own space and the space of others. Our kinesphere is like a giant bubble that surrounds our body. It can expand or shrink, depending on how much space is available to move in and how close to others we feel comfortable being in any given situation.

Young people who are exposed to the concept of Place will find it easier to move in the vicinity of others without bumping or crashing. By giving them the option to move in one spot and encouraging them to find empty spaces as they visualize their own kinesphere and the kinespheres of others, they become more aware of their placement in the room and more responsible in their relationships to other movers.

Idea for Exploring: Have students stand in self space, facing a partner. The leader will move slowly in self space while the partner mirrors (copies) their movements. Both students will dance away from each other in general space, then return to mirroring with the second partner as leader. This works best with a piece of music which has alternating phrases (see Discography).

Size:

Big, Medium, Little

As we move in self or general space we can vary the amount of area our movement takes up. Big movements reach far into space with the body parts stretching wide, while little movements stay very close to the center of the body. We change the size of a shape or movement by growing or shrinking. It is important to note that "big" is not synonymous with "tall" — it is possible to make a big shape by lying on the floor with body parts stretched far apart. We can, in the same way, remain standing and be "little" by holding our body parts close together.

Students who naturally do very big movements, often unintentionally knocking things over or hurting others, can learn to be more careful by being given the opportunity to practice small movements. Young people who are shy or timid may find it easier to be more confident and assertive if they have a chance to practice large movements. It is also helpful to practice growing and shrinking; gradating between big and small.

Idea for Exploring: Ask students to dance with very large movements, taking up as much space as possible. Then ask them to imagine that the room is shrinking, and that they have to make their movements smaller and smaller so as not to bump into walls or other people.

Directions:

Forward, Backward, Right, Left, Up, Down

We can move through general space in any of the six directions listed above. Direction is determined by the surface of the body that is leading us through space: the front of the body leads us forward, the back of our body leads us backward, the sides of our body lead us right and left, the top of our body leads us up and the bottom of our body leads us down.

It is important to differentiate "direction" from "facing," which is determined by a place in the room. For example, you might be facing a window, moving forward toward it, but you could also turn your back to the window and move backward to it. You could also turn, face another side of the room and move forward toward the new facing.

Idea for Exploring: Pairs of students stand with one student in front of the other. The leading student moves through the room in varying directions, followed by their partner. The leader always keeps his or her back to the follower,, which requires caution and awareness when moving backward. At your signal or when the music changes the other student becomes the leader.

Levels:

High, Middle, Low

Level determines whether we are close to the ground or far away. Low level movement is very close to the floor. Slithering, creeping (on hands and knees) and rolling are common low level movements. In high level movement the body is at its full height or in the air. Walking on tiptoe, skipping and leaping are examples of high level movement. Middle level movement is movement between low and high. Some examples of middle level movement are walking crouched over, walking on one's knees with the body upright or "crab-walking" (hands and feet on the floor, stomach toward the ceiling).

We can also change levels as we move. Rising is the action of changing from low level to high and sinking is the action of changing from high level to low.

Idea for Exploring: Have students practice moving on the opposite level of a partner. If one person is moving at a high level, the other must move at a low level. Either student may change levels at any time, challenging their partner to stay alert and be ready to switch levels.

Pathways:

Straight, Curved, Zig-zag

Pathways are the designs our body parts create as they move through space and the designs our feet make as we move across the floor. You might think of your pathway as the "jet stream" you leave behind as you move. When you move in straight pathways you are moving only in straight lines and turning corners sharply. Curved pathways can take the form of circles, spirals or waves. Zig-zag pathways are straight pathways that change direction sharply, as in the contours of lightning or mountain ranges. Pathways can be created on the floor with the feet (or other body parts if moving at a low or middle level) or in the air by moving arms, heads, elbows, etc. Moving in different pathways may evoke varying feelings. For example, moving in a straight pathway might make one feel confident and direct, in a curved pathway confused, and in a zig-zag pathway evasive.

Idea for Exploring: Ask each student to create a simple line-drawing incorporating each of the three pathways, then use the drawing as a map to design movements that travel through the room. This can be done individually or in trios, with each student contributing a different pathway to the drawing. Ask the dancers to name some of the feelings that moving in each pathway evoked for them.

Relationships:

Near, Far, Over, Under, Around, Through, Above, Below, On, Off, etc.

As we move, we are creating relationships between our body parts. We might be moving with all of our body parts near each other, with our arms overhead, or with our hands on our hips. In addition, we may choose to create relationships with objects (a chair, a scarf, a balloon) or with other people. Sometimes all three types of relationships may be happening at once!

Relationships can happen in stillness and in movement. For example, you might make a still shape over a scarf or skip around a partner. When having relationships with other movers we can relate to one person (a partner) or a group of people. It is possible for partners or groups to move over, under, around and through each other. Moving in relationship to others requires awareness and cooperation, essential elements in building interpersonal skills.

Idea for Exploring: Have half of the students make frozen shapes in empty spots in the room. When the music begins the remaining students will move over, under, around and through the shapes. When the music stops the dancers will choose one shape to create a relationship with. For example, if the original shape was wide and open, the dancer might make a smaller shape to fit inside. When the music begins again the original shapes become the dancers and the original dancers make new shapes.

QUALITY

The concept area of Quality defines how a movement is performed: slowly or quickly, strongly or lightly, smoothly or sharply, etc. The quality of a movement is affected by the inner image our mind holds while moving (i.e.: "lightly as a feather"). Quality can also be affected by an attitude or feeling (i.e.: feeling luxurious when moving slowly, feeling urgent when moving quickly).

Speed:
Slow, Medium, Quick (or Fast)

The speed or tempo at which your body moves determines how much time it takes you to complete a movement. Some movements tend to be done slowly, such as floating, melting and stretching. Other movements are usually done quickly: running, shaking, spinning. A large number of movements can be done at any speed. For example: walking, turning and twisting could each be done very slowly, extremely quickly or at any speed in between. Each of these movements could also accelerate (get faster and faster) or decelerate (become progressively slower.)

Many young people tend to move quite quickly and find it a challenge to slow down. For this reason, moving at a variety of speeds is important to practice often.

Idea for Exploring: After asking students to explore moving their entire bodies extremely slowly then extremely quickly, ask them to try moving their upper bodies (heads, torso and arms) slowly while moving the lower body (legs and pelvis) quickly. The reverse is even trickier! Ask students to name some situations in which they tend to move quickly and slowly.

Rhythm:
Pulse, Breath, Pattern

Rhythm is the pattern our movements make in time. The rhythm of our movement can be an even pulse, like a heartbeat, or free flowing and varied like our breath. When we divide time into beats of different lengths we create a rhythmic pattern.

Students in the upper elementary grades enjoy and benefit from both analyzing and learning about rhythm and responding freely to music with different rhythms.

Idea for Exploring: Play a simple, repeated rhythmic pattern on a drum, for example: slow, slow, quick, quick, quick, quick (half-note, half-note, quarter, quarter, quarter, quarter). Allow students to spontaneously create movement patterns that relate to the rhythm. One student's movement might be: twist, twist, jump, jump, jump, jump. Another student's response might be: Curl, stretch, turn, turn, slash, slash. After most students seem to have created a satisfying pattern, try again with a new rhythm.

Have students dance freely to the rhythms of music from different cultures. Have them discuss how their movement varied with each new rhythm.

Weight:
Strong, Light

The quality of Weight defines how we are using our muscles as we move — either with strength and power or lightly and delicately. There are two ways of moving with strong weight. When we use strong weight actively we contract our muscles and press, pull, punch or slash. When we use strong weight passively our muscles are limp and our bodies are heavy, giving in to the pull of gravity. Light movement requires withholding part of one's weight to produce a delicate, lifted feeling. Examples of light movement are floating, flicking and dabbing. However, many movements can be done either strongly or lightly.

Idea for Exploring: Have pairs of students practice sharing their weight. Standing one to two feet apart and facing each other, students press their palms together and lean into each other. The object is for them to share weight equally without one partner overpowering the other. After mastering this shape the partners can explore sharing weight between other body parts: shoulders, backs, feet, etc.

Energy:
Smooth, Sharp

When our Energy is smooth, our movement is ongoing; without stops. Another name for this is "sustained" movement. In contrast, sharp movement is full of quick stops. It can also be called "percussive" or "sudden" movement.

Imagery is often helpful in evoking smooth or sharp movement. Some images for smooth movement might be: painting a wall, clouds floating, birds gliding through the air. Some images for sharp movement might be: punching an enemy, popping a balloon, swatting a fly.

Idea for Exploring: Using balloons, have the students alternate between smooth and sharp movement. They could float, swirl, turn and roll with their balloons smoothly, then bat, tap and kick them sharply. After repeating this exploration several times, challenge them to try it without the balloons! Music with alternating legato and staccato sections works well for this exploration. End the exploration with a discussion of the feelings associated with each type of energy.

Flow:
Free, Bound

When we move with free flow we move with abandon, allowing the movement to flow through our bodies without trying to control or stop it. This might have the sensation of wind or water moving through our bodies and is very smooth and ongoing. Bound flow, by contrast, is very controlled. This could take the form of jerky, robot-like movement or movement with extreme caution or control, as in walking a tightrope. Flow, like all movement qualities, exists on a continuum — absolutely free, moderately free, slightly free to slightly bound, moderately bound, extremely bound.

Some of your students (or yourself!) may tend to move through life in a free-flowing way — "going with the flow" with very little pre-planning, and perhaps being physically reckless. These students can benefit greatly by practicing bound flow movement.

On the other hand, you may also have students who seem very cautious and controlled, afraid to take any risks. These students can open up a great deal through experiencing free-flowing movement. Experiencing the continuum — gradating from one extreme to the other — is helpful for both types of people.

Idea for Exploring: Have students move freely, imagining that a wind is blowing them around the room or that they are a flowing river. Contrast this with moving like robots or machines, keeping their bodies very controlled.

Focus:
Single Focus, Multi-Focus

Focus defines how we direct our attention as we move. When we use single focus, all of our attention is directed toward one thing at a time. We may simply look at one object, place or person or may reach toward it or move toward it. We can change our point of focus very rapidly but as long as we focus on one thing at a time we are using single focus.

When we allow our attention to widen we are using multi-focus. This is when we direct our attention toward many things at once. We might imagine that we are scanning a horizon. Our eyes may look at many places in the room and our body might be turning or weaving in space.

Idea for Exploring: Students mirror a partner in self space (see Idea for Exploring the concept Place), focusing strongly on that partner. Call out a specific point of focus as they dance away from each other through general space (i.e.: "focus on your hand," "focus on the window," "focus on another person," "focus all around the room") When they return to each other the second partner will be the leader for mirroring.

A FINAL NOTE:

Though each concept has been described here separately, the Movement Concepts never function in isolation. Even in the simple act of walking across the room you will be using several different concepts at once: you may be walking in a forward Direction at a high Level and a fast Speed through general Space! The combining of Movement Concepts is what makes the possibilities of movement infinitely creative and exciting.

Chapter Three
Basic Effort Actions

Several of the lessons in this book make use of particular movements which researcher Rudolph von Laban called "Basic Effort Actions." Basic Effort Actions are movements which combine the elements of Weight (strong or light), Focus (single focus or multi-focus) and Speed (slow or quick) in specific configurations (see chart following this chapter). I will describe each of the Basic Effort Actions in detail below, providing imagery which may help you execute the movement. It is suggested that you try each of the movements yourself before guiding your students in exploring them.

The Effort Actions are very closely linked to the expression of emotion, and to each person's individual movement style or "movement signature." As you physically explore each of the actions described opposite, try really exaggerating them or taking them to the extreme. For example, make your float so light that you feel as if you're not even touching the ground; make your punching as strong and quick as possible. As you exaggerate a movement notice what feeling you associate with it. Does floating make you feel "spaced out?" Does punching make you feel aggressive or full of rage? Also notice what type of person you imagine you might be as you do each movement. Does floating make you feel like a person who is out of touch with reality? Does punching make you imagine you are someone who is very powerful and goal oriented? Each individual will naturally associate different feelings and images with each of the Basic Effort Actions, though the connotations of some of the actions are universal (such as the association of hostility with punching.)

WHAT ARE BASIC EFFORT ACTIONS?

float — a float is a movement which is light, slow and uses multi-focus. You may feel as if your body is barely touching the earth; as if you are drifting weightlessly. Let your attention wander to take in many parts of the room. Images: balloons, clouds, smoke, astronaut on the moon, seaweed.

glide — a glide is a movement which is light, slow and single-focused. You might feel as if you are weightlessly moving toward a specific point in the room. Images: birds, ice-skating, duck moving across the surface of a lake, smoothing a sheet, finger-painting.

flick — a flick is a movement which is light, quick and multi-focused. You may move as if you are lightly flipping air away from you. Each flick has a definite initiation, but is not directed toward a specific point in space. Images: getting rid of mosquitoes, twitching, dismissing an idea, shaking water off your body, lightly jerking.

dab — a dab is a movement which is light, quick and single-focused. You may feel as if you are touching something precisely or cautiously. The end of the movement will have more emphasis than the beginning. Images: making polka dots with finger-paint, testing the temperature of water, patting something lightly, tapping on a window.

slash — a slash is a movement which is strong, quick and multi-focused. You might feel as if you are powerfully slicing a diagonal line through space. The end of the slash will not be directed toward any particular point. Images: flinging something away from you, a knife slicing the space, throwing open a curtain, whipping a horse.

punch — a punch is a movement which is strong, quick and single-focused. You may move as if you are thrusting a body part powerfully through a wall. The energy of the punch will be directed toward a single point in space. Images: fighting, pushing someone quickly away, kicking, jabbing, battering down a door.

wring — a wring is a movement which is strong, slow and multi-focused. You may feel as if you are strongly squeezing and twisting. Images: wringing out a washcloth, wringing someone's neck (!), turning away from a strong wind, pulling taffy.

press — a press is a movement which is strong, slow and single focused. You might feel as if you are pushing something toward a particular place in space. Images: pushing a heavy rock, crushing something underfoot, cutting through a mound of dense clay, lifting a weight, squeezing a giant pair of pliers.

As you become more familiar with the basic effort actions you will notice which ones you tend to gravitate toward in your own everyday movements, as well as which ones are most commonly used by particular students. Everyone has one or two basic effort actions which they tend to use most often, so it is interesting and challenging to "try on" the actions that are least natural to you.

TABLE OF BASIC EFFORT ACTIONS

	WEIGHT		FOCUS		SPEED	
	Strong	Light	Single	Multi	Slow	Quick
float		X		X	X	
glide		X	X		X	
flick		X		X		X
dab		X	X			X
slash	X			X		X
punch	X		X			X
wring	X			X	X	
press	X		X		X	

Chapter Four
How to Use this Book

If you are like many classroom teachers, the lessons in this book may be very different from the types of activities you usually engage in with your students. Or, if you are lucky enough to be working in a school or district where teachers are supported in integrating the arts into the curriculum, this type of material may be more familiar to you. In either case this chapter will help guide you in determining how these movement-based lessons can fit into your existing curriculum, how to prepare your students to engage in movement activities successfully, and how to most effectively present the lessons in this book.

WHEN TO USE THE *MOVING IS RELATING* LESSONS IN YOUR CLASSROOM

There are two possible methods for integrating the lessons in this book into your classroom. You may decide that you would like to emphasize intrapersonal and interpersonal awareness with your students, and present a lesson from this book on a weekly or bi-weekly basis. Note that the lessons do not necessarily need to be presented in a particular order — you may sequence them in any way you choose to create the curriculum that best suits your needs and the needs of your students.

Another possible way to use this book is to have the lessons available to present when interpersonal issues arise in your classroom. For example, if you notice that communica-tion tends to be a problem among your students you might choose several lessons from the "Communication" section to present. Or, if you are planning to have your students work together on a project, you might present one of the lessons on cooperation or collabo-ration to prepare them for the process.

PREPARING YOUR STUDENTS FOR MOVEMENT-BASED LESSONS

The majority of the lessons in this book can be successfully presented to students who have little or no experience in creative move-ment or dance. However, your students will enjoy the lessons more and be able to explore them in more depth if they have at least a rudimentary knowledge of the Movement Concepts. For this reason it is highly recom-mended that you take the time with your stu-dents during the year to experience and explore the Movement Concepts described in the previous chapter.

The theory and methodology of teaching Creative Dance is certainly too large a subject to be covered in this chapter and several excellent books have been written on the sub-ject, most notably Anne Green Gilbert's *Creative Dance for All Ages* (see Bibliography). I will simply get you started with a format for planning Creative Dance lessons. Two sample lesson plans can be found in the Appendices. Many more lesson plans can be found in Gilbert's book.

A thirty to sixty minute Creative Dance lesson for third to sixth graders should include the following components:

1. Warm-up

An opportunity for students to warm up their muscles through light aerobic movements such as stretching, curling, bending, twisting, swinging and shaking.

2. Concept Introduction

Introduce students to one of the Movement Concepts described in the previous chapter. Have them say the concept words while briefly experiencing the movements or shapes those words describe. For example, when being introduced to the concept Size the students would say the words "big," "medium" and "little" while making shapes of those sizes with their bodies.

3. Concept Exploration

In this section of the lesson students have an opportunity to initially explore the concept and discover how it affects their movement. This can be done individually, in partners or groups, with or without the use of props (scarves, crepe paper streamers, balloons, etc.). There is a suggested concept exploration activity for each Movement Concept under the heading *Idea for Exploring* in Chapter 2, "What Are Movement Concepts?"

4. Skill Development

In a well-rounded Creative Dance class, it is important to include not only opportunities for creative exploration, but also activities for the development of physical skills. The skill development section of the lesson could include one or more of the following:

Rhythm skills: developing a sense of rhythm through playing musical instruments to a beat, moving to rhythmic chants or performing movement to counts.

Locomotor and Non-locomotor skills: practicing skills such as skipping, turning, sliding, floating, slashing and so on.

Leaping: practicing the skill of leaping is fun and exciting and encourages development of both sides of the body through taking off from one foot and landing on the other. You may want to begin by asking students to leap over stacked objects such as milk cartons or boxes, then take the objects away when they are no longer needed as visual cues.

Movement combinations: practicing a sequence of movements or a "dance." This requires students to remember a sequence and to learn to link movements together. A movement combination could be a folk or square dance, a popular dance or a dance you create by making a sentence of locomotor and non-locomotor words. An example of such a dance might be: "skip… melt…roll…rise…turn…leap." These movements could be performed to specific counts or with the students' own timing.

It is important to teach skills by referring to the concept introduced at the beginning of the lesson. For example, if you are teaching the concept Level (High, Middle, Low) you might have the students practice rolling low and leaping high, then do a simple dance that changes levels. Activities such as these will develop skills that reinforce the Movement Concept.

Improvisation or Choreography

Conclude your lesson by allowing students to use the concept they have learned to express themselves creatively through improvising — performing movement spontaneously, or choreographing — pre-planning movement. In a lesson on the concept Pathways (Straight, Curved, Zig-zag) students might improvise in response to famous works of art, spontaneously dancing the Pathways they see. Or, for choreography, you might give small groups art reproductions and ask them to plan and perform movements based on the lines in the paintings.

Students in Grades 3-6 will enjoy and benefit from having a complete Creative Dance class, as described above, once or twice a week with the focus on a different Movement Concept each week. If you feel that this is an impossibility for you to provide, it will be extremely helpful to, at the very least, do the activity described under the heading *Idea for Exploring* in Chapter 2, "What Are Movement Concepts?" for each concept, introducing one or two concepts a week.

USING THE *MOVING IS RELATING* LESSONS

Once you have familiarized yourself with the introductory material in Chapters 1-5 and have begun to introduce your students to the Movement Concepts, you are ready to start using the *Moving Is Relating* lessons. The lessons are divided into two main parts. Part I: Developing Intrapersonal Awareness deals with self-knowledge and self-perception. Part II: Developing Interpersonal Skills deals with the skills involved in relating to others including communicating effectively, establishing trust and working cooperatively.

Each lesson contains important information under the following headings:

Topic

The specific topic of each lesson can be found in its title at the top of the lesson's first page. Once you have chosen a lesson you wish to present, read it carefully several times. Ask yourself if there are any preparatory experiences you might want to provide to make the lesson as rich and successful as possible. Would it be helpful for the students to hear or read a particular short story before doing the movement activity? To see a video? To view a painting or photograph or discuss a classroom incident or current event? Providing your students with applicable background material helps "fuel" them for self-expression.

Type of Movement Activity

This heading tells you how the material in the lesson will be presented and how the students will be grouped. There are three types of movement activities included in this book:

Shapes: Activities which are shape oriented, with very little movement through space.

Improvisational Exploration: Teacher-guided activities which involve spontaneous movement through space.

Choreography: Activities in which the teacher presents a structure, then acts as an advisor as the students work in groups to plan and execute their own movement sequences or "dances" within that structure. The choreographic activity concludes with an opportunity for each group to perform their work and receive positive comments from their audience.

Each type of movement activity is presented in one of the following groupings:

Individual: Individual students explore an idea without necessarily relating to others, though there are others moving in the space with them.

Partner: Two students work together to create shapes, explore an idea or create choreography.

Small Group: Groups of three to six students work together.

Large Group: Six or more students work together.

In general, the simplest lessons are those involving individual improvisational exploration because there is a minimal need for students to cooperate, collaborate or adapt to each other. The most complex lessons are those involving large group choreography because they require large groups of students to collaborate creatively in planning a movement study.

Related Concepts

This heading tells you which of the Movement Concepts described in Chapter 2 are most involved in the execution of the movement in each lesson. These concepts may or may not be explicitly referred to during the lesson. This heading is provided to give you an opportunity to prepare your students for the lesson's creative demands by introducing them to one or more of the related Movement Concepts.

Materials / Preparation

This heading lets you know if any specific materials or preparation are needed or suggested in order to teach the lesson.

Musical Suggestions

Many of the lessons in this book can be done without music. However, music is very motivating for movement and can help students feel more involved and less self-conscious.

Although a few of the lessons suggest specific musical selections, most lessons can be successfully presented using any selection from the Discography at the end of this book as background music. Feel free to choose one of the selections listed, or to use a personal favorite of your own. Be aware that, in general, New Age, classical, ethnic or folk music are more conducive to creative movement than popular music, which tends to elicit stereotyped "hip" movement from students at this age. You will also find instrumental music to be more effective than music with lyrics.

Space Requirements

It is a sad truth that adequate space for movement activities in the typical elementary school building is minimal. It is frustrating to note that, while most schools and districts are willing to spend thousands of dollars on computer equipment, providing space for children to use their most natural learning resource — their own bodies — is not something most budget planners and administrators would even consider. Therefore it unfortunately becomes the responsibility of the classroom teacher to adjust, adapt and advocate for change in this vital area.

The information under this heading tells you whether the lesson requires a large, open space such as an empty classroom, gym, stage or outdoor area, or can be done in an open area (the front and / or aisles) of the regular classroom. Though I have tried to adapt as many lessons as possible to the space of the regular classroom, some activities simply lose their impact if the students do not have ample room to move. After all, learning through movement requires...moving!

What can you do to find or create the space you need? Here are a few possibilities:

• Be aware of all the open spaces in your school and when they are available, if even for half an hour. Try the music room, gym, lunchroom, stage, computer lab, library, etc.

- Do a movement activity outdoors on a mild day.

- Create a routine for clearing as much space as possible in your classroom. Challenge students to rearrange the furniture in record amounts of time (and put it back when the lesson is over.)

- If all of these suggestions fail and you find yourself stuck in a regular classroom with the desks in rows, try the following:

- Do the movement activity moving up and down the aisles.

- Whenever possible, change general space (traveling) movement to self space (stationary) movement.

- Have only half or even a third of the students participate in an activity with the rest of the class watching. Repeat the activity again with the other group(s) moving or rotate giving students a turn to participate on different days.

- Assign students a choreographic structure and send small groups into hallways or other areas of the school building to create their dances or movement studies.

Time Required

This heading gives you an approximate idea of how much time it will take to present the lesson, including approximately ten minutes of discussion. Lengths of the lessons in this book range between fifteen and forty-five minutes. Your actual presentation time may vary from the approximate time given depending on your personal teaching style,

the responses of your students and the amount of time you wish to spend discussing the lesson.

Introducing the Lesson

The lesson's introduction gives you and your students background information about the lesson's topic. Feel free to read the introduction to the students as it is written, to paraphrase it or to write your own. The important thing is to be sure the students have a context for the activity they are about to engage in.

Teaching the Lesson

Although the lessons are written in a word-for-word scripted form they are actually meant to be used as guides. They are written as scripts to show you one possible way of guiding the students through each lesson. Though you are welcome to read a lesson word for word it is hoped that you will adapt the manner of presentation to your teaching style and to the particular needs of your students.

Be aware as you teach the lessons that each question you pose or direction you give will elicit widely varying responses from your students. For example, if you ask "How will your body grow into an angry shape?" one student may respond by strongly pressing as he rises, another might pop up from the ground suddenly and a third might punch the air while changing level. All of these responses are valid, though they are very different. When guiding children in a movement activity your job is not to get them to respond "correctly," but to respond appropriately and creatively.

Another responsibility you have as a guide while students are exploring movement is to continually make them aware of possible choices. During any part of a lesson that asks you to allow the students time to explore an idea through movement you can greatly aid your students by asking them questions based on the list of Movement Concepts and the partial listing of Locomotor and Non-Locomotor Movements, both found at the beginning of Chapter 2. Here are examples of the kinds of questions you might ask aloud as students are moving: "Could you try that movement on a different Level?...in a different Direction?... Could you make the movement much larger? ...much smaller? Is it possible to change the Speed of the movement?"

Another way to encourage creative response as students are moving is to point out the interesting choices you see, for example: "Mary is really using her arms in a strong way! I see David turning as he floats. Joey and Rob are making a shape together." These kinds of statements not only acknowledge the students who are making creative choices; they also suggest new possibilities to the other students.

Questions for Discussion

Each lesson concludes with a series of questions to be discussed by the students. You may choose to discuss these questions as a class, to break into pairs or small groups or to have students reflect on the questions individually and answer them in journal form. You may use all of the questions for a given lesson, or select just a few to discuss in more depth. Of course, you are also free to make up questions of your own.

The purpose of the questions is not to lead your students toward an answer or point of view that you feel to be correct, but to actually engage them in reflecting honestly on how they operate in the world and in relation to other people. If you, as a teacher, are able to provide an open, non-judgmental forum for your students to express their perceptions and opinions on these topics, the depth and

maturity of the conclusions they reach will most likely exceed your expectations. Furthermore, the very process of discussion will provide valuable learning in the areas of communication, trust and self-expression.

Troubleshooting

Sometimes, despite your best efforts, you may find yourself in the middle of a movement activity that seems "stuck": the students just don't know what to do. Before you panic and call a halt to the activity, try the following:

• Give an example or demonstration of the kind of responses that are possible.

• Simplify a complex lesson by only doing one part of it.

• Do a choreographic activity as a whole class, with your guidance, rather than breaking the class into groups.

• Let students know how they can get ideas when they feel stuck: look at the Movement Concepts chart and/or watch other students — in creative movement "copying" is great!

• For more on managing movement activities, see Chapter 5, "Managing Movement."

Assessment

At some point after the lesson is completed you will want to asses its effectiveness. I suggest waiting at least an hour or two before making an assessment because by that time you will be able to be more objective and less self-critical.

First, think about what went *well* in the lesson. When were the students particularly engaged? What were some really creative responses you observed? At what points did you feel that they really "got" the content of the lesson?

Next, take a look at any difficulties or problems you encountered and try to determine their cause. Were your directions to the students unclear? Did you neglect to direct the transitions from one part of the lesson to the next? Did you allow a student's negative behavior to garner too much of your attention? Being as specific as you can about the cause of any difficulties will help you avoid them in the future.

Last of all, just as you praise your students for striving for their highest potential, treat yourself well — no matter how the lesson went — for doing something that is new and challenging for you. You will find, over time, that using movement as a teaching tool seems less overwhelming and becomes, instead, vastly rewarding to both yourself and your students.

Chapter Five
Managing Movement

When they imagine leading their students in a movement activity many teachers envision a scene of noisy, directionless chaos. Unfortunately, the fear of such an occurrence often prevents these teachers from even attempting to use movement as a teaching tool. While a misdirected movement activity could certainly lead to noisy confusion, a well-planned, well executed lesson leads to engaged, motivated activity.

It is natural for a class to look and sound less controlled when engaging in movement than in some other educational processes. That is because the students are enthusiastic and excited and are actively involved with the content of the lesson and with each other. In other words, they're responding exactly the way we, as educators, should want them to respond. But because the standards for student behavior, formulated in a past generation, say that students are not learning unless they are sitting quietly at their desks, it is difficult for us to view this less controlled situation as a positive learning environment. We have to change our idea of what learning looks like in order to embrace movement as an appropriate educational activity.

Just as we must teach children the rules of a game before they can play it safely and successfully, we must educate them about *how* to engage in movement. In most classrooms, movement activities are not part of the usual school day. There is no reason that students in such classrooms would know how to behave during a movement-based lesson. But often teachers who have never introduced movement before will try it once, then give up altogether because their students did not respond in the way they expected. This is as unfair to the students as it would be to give long division problems to a class that had never been introduced to long division, then say "never again" when they failed to solve the problems correctly!

This chapter will give you some general guidelines for leading your students in movement activities. Keep in mind, as you read, that "practice makes perfect" and the more you use movement as a teaching tool the more positively and appropriately your students will respond.

Set clear expectations

As in any teaching situation, it is of vital importance to set clear boundaries and expectations for behavior. It is often helpful to have your students collaborate with you in creating a set of rules specifically for movement. An example of such a set of rules might be:

Listen and follow directions.
Move carefully, touch gently.
Make kind, positive comments.
Do excellent work.

It is best to state rules positively rather than telling students what they should not do. You may also want to set behavioral expectations specific to the space you are working in, such as "move only on the floor of the gym; stay off the bleachers." The clearer you can be at the outset about what kind of behavior you expect the more safe your students will feel and the more positively they will respond.

It is useful to have a "freeze" signal; a signal which immediately stops all speaking and activity. A beat on a drum or tambourine works well for this purpose. It is a good idea to set up the freeze signal at the beginning of the very first movement activity you do with a group and to give the students a chance to practice responding to it several times.

Give clear directions

It is very possible for a movement activity to fail because directions were not given clearly. Giving clear directions means telling students exactly what they are expected to do. The lessons in this book have been scripted so as to make the directions to students as clear as possible. It is important that students are always told where to go to begin a new activity and what to do when they get there. They need to be told how to engage in the activity and what to do when the activity has been completed.

The most common place for management to break down is in the transition between two sections of a lesson. For example, if the whole class does an improvisation and the students are then asked to get into groups to work on choreography, the transition from working as a class to working in groups could be problematic. It is important to plan exactly how the transition will take place and to communicate that plan to students.

Organizing groups

To organize students into pairs or small groups you may find it simplest to let them quickly make their own choices by giving them a task such as "by the time I count to ten, please find a friend (or two or three friends) and make a connected shape." Putting a time limitation on choosing groups prevents students from belaboring the process.

In some classes, due to interpersonal issues between students, asking them to choose their own partners or groups can be problematic. In this situation you may want to organize your students into appropriate groupings before beginning the lesson and read or post your list as part of preparing for an activity. Another possibility is to draw numbers out of a hat and allow groups to be chosen randomly.

Dividing your class in half can be accomplished simply by drawing an imaginary line through the middle of the group. Or, you may choose to have students "count off" 1's and 2's to make the grouping more random. The most important thing to remember in organizing groups is that it should happen quickly and matter-of-factly rather than becoming a major focus of the lesson.

Acknowledge appropriate behavior

One of the best ways to manage student behavior in any learning situation is to acknowledge appropriate behavior when you see it. It is just as important to praise positive behavior as it is to praise creativity. Your students yearn for your attention. Once they discover that behaving appropriately is the way to get that attention, they will eagerly exhibit the behavior you seek. Comments such as "I really appreciate the way Billy is listening to my directions" or "Susan and Jesse are being very gentle with each other as they move together" let all of your students know what kind of behavior you value.

Acknowledging appropriate behavior is most effective when it is coupled with ignoring negative behavior. Although it can be extremely difficult to ignore a student who is behaving inappropriately it is crucial to successful classroom management. Try "catching" a difficult student behaving well — even for a second — and acknowledge him or her immediately.

Discussing

Handling non-participation

A major concern for teachers who have never tried movement activities with their class is that their students "won't do it." My experience is that children of this age *love* to move and dance, and that most will gladly participate when given an opportunity. Boys, especially, are thrilled to have a chance to move when they discover that large, energetic movements are just as valued as graceful, delicate ones.

While most children participate in movement activities readily, it is not uncommon to have one or two students in a class who may initially resist joining in. Sometimes, if a child is timid or shy or comes from a family or cultural background where physical expression is not encouraged, he or she may feel threatened and overwhelmed when invited into a movement experience. It is usually best to let such students enter the activity when they feel ready. Allow them to watch for awhile so they can determine that the situation is physically, emotionally and socially safe. Most students who are initially timid will eventually participate eagerly.

Another type of non-participation stems from a student's desire to enter into a power struggle with you or to impress his or her peers by being too "cool" to participate. In this case it is best to simply state that participation is mandatory, just as it is for math or language arts. Your attitude carries a lot of weight in this situation: if *you* value movement as much as you value the other curricular subjects your students are more likely to do so as well.

The bottom line in cases of non-participation is to use your good judgment and intuition to determine whether, in each individual situation, it is best to allow the child to be an observer or to ask him or her to rise to the challenge of full participation.

Managing the noise level

Students will naturally be more verbal when engaging in a movement activity than they are when sitting at their desks listening, reading or writing. It is important to determine whether the noise level is appropriate, as when they are talking with classmates to solve a movement problem, or when the noise level is higher than it needs to be. Many students have difficulty moving without speaking or making sounds because the only other time they have a chance to move is on the playground where shouting and yelling are the norm. They simply need training and practice in how to move quietly.

I find it useful to demonstrate to the class that movement is a way to communicate and express oneself without sound. Ask them to show you, with their bodies, that they are excited…angry…sad…surprised. Encourage them to put the intensity of those feelings into their bodies without using their voices. Last of all, be sure to praise them whenever they are particularly successful in moving quietly.

Movement is motivating

Although you may find it challenging, initially, to manage movement activities with your class, over time you will find that movement becomes its own motivation. Your students will want to behave well because they will want you to keep providing them with movement experiences! Letting your students know that their involvement in movement is important to you is your most effective management tool.

PART ONE

INTRAPERSONAL AWARENESS

In order to truly connect with others, one must have an awareness of oneself. This includes knowing who you are and what makes you unique as an individual, identifying and taking responsibility for your thoughts, emotions and actions and defining clearly the boundaries that separate you from other human beings. Educational theorist Howard Gardner labeled this type of self-knowledge the "intrapersonal intelligence."

The lessons in this section of the book will help students develop, through movement, a beginning awareness of who they are and how they relate to the world around them.

Section A: Identity
Section B: Emotions
Section C: The Self in Action

Section A: Identity

A person's identity is what makes them unique and separate from other individuals. There are many ways to describe and define a person's identity: on a surface level their name serves to define their identity and their fingerprints may be used as a form of identification. In our society we often think of a person's work or hobbies as part of their identity, along with their race, religion, culture or nationality. We may use a person's physical characteristics, their personality or way of relating to others in describing their identity.

In the following lesson your students will discover an exciting way of looking at a person's identity called their "Movement Signature."

Lesson 1: Movement Signature

Type of Movement Activity:
Individual Improvisational Exploration

Related Movement Concepts:
Basic Effort Actions (see Chapter 3)

Materials / Preparation:
This lesson focuses on Rudolph von Laban's "Efforts":

float	glide
flick	dab
slash	punch
wring	press

It would be wise to familiarize yourself with the characteristics of these movements by reading Chapter 3: Basic Effort Actions before presenting this lesson. Be sure to try each movement yourself so you can describe it effectively to

your students. It will be helpful to have the names of these movements posted during the lesson.

Musical Suggestions:
It is best to do this lesson without music to facilitate each child finding his or her own individual movement style.

Space Required:
This lesson can easily take place in the regular classroom with students either traveling through the aisles between desks or remaining stationary behind their seats. It is also an exciting lesson to present in a large, open space such as an empty classroom, gym or outdoor area.

Time Required:
Approximately 15 minutes.

Introduction:

Each of you is a unique person, different from every other human being on this earth. Just as no two people look exactly the same or speak in the same way, so do no two human beings have exactly the same way of moving their bodies. Each person's unique, special way of moving is called their "movement signature."

Lesson:

Find a place to stand where you can stretch in all directions without touching anyone. *(If this lesson is to be done in the classroom without traveling, ask students to stand behind their chairs.)* I'm going to introduce you to eight different movements called Basic Effort Actions. As you try each movement, notice which ones feel very comfortable and familiar to you. These movements are probably a part of your personal movement signature. Also notice which ones make you move in a new or unfamiliar way.

The first movement we'll try is **floating**. Floating feels very light and slow, like a cloud or a feather drifting in the breeze. See if your hands can float...your legs...your head. When you float you'll probably find yourself turning and looking at many different things.

(Allow students approximately one minute to explore floating.)

Next we'll try a movement called **gliding**. You might imagine that you are an airplane or seagull gliding through the air. Try reaching your arms as you glide. Gliding is smooth and it should feel as if you're going somewhere even if you're standing in one place.

(Allow students approximately one minute to explore gliding.)

Gliding

Our next movement is called **flicking**. It is a quick, light movement like you might use to flick a fly or mosquito away from you. Try flicking with your hands...your head...a shoulder...a foot.

(Allow students approximately one minute to explore flicking.)

The next movement, **dabbing**, will feel like you're putting little dabs of paint into the air. Try dabbing with your toes on the floor...with your fingers in the air...with your nose!

(Allow students approximately one minute to explore dabbing.)

Now we'll do a sharp, strong movement called **slashing**. You might feel like your arm is a knife slicing the air. Try slashing with your leg...or even your head.

(Allow students approximately one minute to explore slashing.)

Next, let's try **punching**. You can imagine that you're punching holes in the air. Be sure you don't punch another person. Can your elbows punch...your knees...your hips?

(Allow students approximately one minute to explore punching.)

Now we'll do some **wringing**. Imagine that you have a wet towel, and you want to twist it to squeeze all of the water out. You will be using a lot of muscles, and your movement will be very smooth. Can you wring up high...down low...on a middle level?

(Allow students approximately one minute to explore wringing.)

Last of all, let's **press**. Imagine you're pushing against a heavy rock. Your movement will be slow and strong. Try pressing in front of you...behind...up....down.

(Allow students approximately one minute to explore pressing.)

Now take a moment to decide which of those eight movements felt most comfortable and familiar to you. *(NOTE: It is helpful to have all eight movements written on the board for students to refer to.)*

I'm going to name all eight Basic Effort Actions again. When I name the one you felt most comfortable doing, go ahead and do the movement again. When you are not moving watch the other students carefully.

> *(Say all eight effort words, allowing approximately twenty seconds between each word for students to move. You may want to have students sit, then stand and move when they hear their chosen word, or to have all students stand at the edge of the room and come to the center to move when their word is called.)*

Now take a moment to decide which word felt most unfamiliar or uncomfortable to you. Which of these eight movements do you almost never do?

> *(Repeat the process above, this time having students move when their most unfamiliar movement is called. After all eight words have been called, and all students have tried their most unfamiliar movement, ask the class to take their seats for discussion.)*

Questions for Discussion:

- The movement you chose as most comfortable and familiar to you is probably a part of your movement signature — your own unique, habitual way of moving. Who would like to share which movement they felt most comfortable with, and what they imagined or felt as they did that movement?

- When you watched other students move, did they ever move differently from each other even when they were doing the same effort word? How would you describe the differences?

- How did it feel to do the movement that was most unfamiliar to you?

- Can you think of a time in your life when you were asked to do something new and unfamiliar, something that was really a "stretch" for you? What happened? How did it feel? What did you learn?

Variations:

Ask students to make a vocal sound as they perform each movement. This will help them express the emotion that each particular movement makes them feel.

Extended Activities:

Ask students to watch people's movements over the next few days, paying particular attention to any of the eight Basic Effort Actions they notice.

Section B: Emotions

All human beings share the experience of feeling emotions. However, particularly in Western cultures, we tend to view some emotions as being more desirable or comfortable than others. While we all long to experience joy and excitement, for example, many of us would rather not be required to experience anger, despair or frustration.

It is vital for young people to develop an awareness of their emotions, as doing so facilitates their ability to relate to others. When one has experienced an emotion it is much easier to empathize with another who is experiencing similar feelings. It is also important for students to realize that their emotions are their own and that someone else may have quite different feelings, even in the same circumstance.

The following lessons will facilitate students in using movement to identify and express emotions, and to discuss those emotions with their peers.

Lesson 2: Identifying Emotions

Type of Movement Activity:
Individual Improvisational Exploration

Related Movement Concepts:
Basic Effort Actions (see Chapter 3)

Materials / Preparations:
chalkboard and chalk
or butcher paper and felt pens
one sheet of paper per student
one pen or pencil per student

This lesson focuses on the Basic Effort Actions described in Chapter 3, and in *Lesson 1: Movement Signature*. It is helpful, but not necessary, for students to have experienced Lesson 1 before doing this lesson.

Musical Suggestions:
It is best to present this lesson without music, as music tends to affect the emotions of the listener.

Space Requirements:
This lesson can easily take place in the regular classroom with students either traveling through the aisles between desks or remaining stationary behind their seats. It is also an exciting lesson to present in a large, open space such as an empty classroom, gym or outdoor area.

Time Required:
Approximately 20 minutes.

Introduction:

One experience that all human beings share is that of having feelings or emotions. Some emotions, such as joy and excitement, are feelings most people enjoy. Other emotions, like anger or sadness, may be more uncomfortable.

Lesson:

Let's begin by listing as many different emotions as we can think of on the board. Raise your hand if you'd like to name an emotion, and I'll write it down.

(Write the emotions named by the students. They may require some coaching to come up with subtler emotions such as suspicion, confusion or boredom.)

Find an empty spot to stand where you can stretch in all directions without touching anyone. *(If this lesson is to be done in the classroom without traveling, ask students to stand behind their chairs.)* I'm going to call out eight different movements called "Basic Effort Actions." Try doing each of the movements with your body, and notice any emotions you feel as you are moving. Don't try to *make* yourself feel an emotion, just move and see if an emotion comes to you.

(Call out and briefly describe each one of the effort movements, as in Lesson 1:

> *float*
> *glide*
> *flick*
> *dab*
> *slash*
> *punch*
> *wring*
> *press*

See Lesson 1 for descriptions of each movement. Allow students approximately one minute to explore each word before moving on to the next one. After completing the exploration of a word, ask students to glance at the board and notice any of the listed emotions they may have experienced.

After all eight Basic Effort Actions have been explored, ask students to take their seats.)

Now take out your paper and pencil. I'm going to say each effort word again. As I say it, write it down. Next to the word, write any emotions you felt while doing that word.

(Say all eight Basic Effort Action words again. You may want to write each word on the board to alleviate any difficulties with spelling. Each student's completed list should look something like this:

> *float — happy*
> *glide — courageous*
> *flick — irritated*
> *dab — nervous*
> *slash — excited*
> *punch — angry*
> *wring — frustrated*
> *press — confident*

Of course, each student's list of emotions will be different.)

Questions for Discussion:

• Who would like to share what emotion they felt when doing the word "float"? Why do you imagine that it made you feel that way? (Repeat this question with other words on the list.)

• Did each person experience the same emotions for each effort word? Why not?

• Why do you think some words brought up similar emotions in many people? (For example, many students will probably list "angry" as a response to the word "punch.")

• Do people all experience the same emotions at the same time? Can you think of a time when you felt one way and the person you were with felt differently? (You may want to give an example from your own life.)

• Are there certain events that do tend to make people feel similar emotions? What's an event that would make most people feel joyful? Angry? Sad?

Variations:

As noted in Lesson 1, you could invite students to make vocal sounds while performing each word. Be aware that, while some students greatly enjoy vocalizing, others may feel self-conscious and inhibited. It is best to make vocalizing a choice rather than a requirement.

Extended Activities:

Print one Basic Effort Action on each of eight 3x5 cards. Print emotion words on cards of a different color. Make a game of pulling an emotion card and an Effort Action card and putting the two together in movement, i.e.: "happy slash" or "frustrated float." The unexpected combinations will give students further experience in the range of possible emotional expressions. It's also a lot of fun!

Lesson 3: Changing Emotions

Type of Movement Activity:
Individual Improvisational Exploration

Related Movement Concepts:
Place (self space, general space)
Basic Effort Actions (see Chapter 3)

Materials / Preparation
Chalkboard or butcher paper with the following words written on it:

> sad
> angry
> bored
> afraid
> suspicious

chalk or marker
Note: This lesson is designed to follow *Lesson 2: Identifying Emotions.*

Musical Suggestions:
This lesson works most effectively without music.

Space Required:
This lesson requires students to travel from one side of a room to another, and therefore works best in an open space such as an empty classroom, gym, lunchroom, stage or defined outdoor area. In the regular classroom, allow as many students to travel at once as space will permit. Let different students take a turn to move each time.

Time Required:
Approximately 15 minutes.

Introduction:

Our emotions are constantly changing. Sometimes the changes happen very quickly: you may be feeling really happy, then something happens that makes you sad. Some changes happen over a longer period of time. A person who often feels timid and shy may work for years to be more courageous and confident. It is important to feel each of our emotions fully, but we don't have to worry that an uncomfortable feeling will last forever.

Lesson:

I've written five different emotion words on the board. Let's look at the first one: sad. If a person were feeling sad and something happened to change that feeling, what new emotion might the person feel?

(Allow students to discuss this briefly, then write down one of the answers they suggest. Repeat this process for each of the five words. There are no "right" answers, though it is probably more

helpful for students to experience moving from a "negative" emotion such as sadness to a "positive" emotion such as joy. Your finished list might look like this:

> *sad — happy*
> *angry — peaceful*
> *bored — excited*
> *afraid — courageous*
> *suspicious — trusting*

When your list is complete, ask students to stand side by side against a wall.)

We'll be traveling in straight lines from here to the opposite side of the room. We'll start with the first pair of words, and move from sad to joyful (or whichever emotion your class listed opposite the word "sad.") You will start traveling across the room with movements that express sadness to you. You might use one of the effort words that made you feel sad: float, glide, flick, dab, slash, punch, wring or press. Or you might have another way of expressing sadness in movement. Perhaps your movement will be very slow. Perhaps you will be focusing downward.

Somewhere near the middle of the room, change your sad movements to joyful ones. Find your own way to express joy — put it into many different body parts, let it change the speed or level of your movement. By the time you reach the opposite side of the room, your movement should have changed completely.

(Allow students to complete this task. Repeat with the four other emotion changes from your list. When the four changes are completed ask students to take their seats for discussion. NOTE: In a regular classroom, allow only a few pairs of students to travel at once. Give new pairs of students a chance to move for each emotion pair.)

Questions for Discussion:

• Was it easy or difficult to change your movement from expressing one emotion to another?

• Did you change your movement gradually or suddenly?

• Which change on the list was the easiest for you to make? Which was the most difficult?

• When in your life have your emotions changed quickly? Can you describe how that happened?

• Has there ever been a time when your feelings about someone or something changed more gradually?

• Can you control your emotions, or do they happen beyond your control?

Variations:

Have students work in pairs standing across the room from each other. As they trade places, partners will "exchange" emotions.

Extended Activities:

Ask students to select one of the emotional changes on the list and write a short story in which a person has one of the emotions at the beginning of the story and changes to the other by the end.

Excitement

Lesson 4: Emotion Garden

Type of Movement Activity:
Group Improvisational Exploration

Related Movement Concepts:
Shape (straight, curved, angular, twisted)
Place (self space, general space)

Materials / Preparation:
It will be helpful to have some different emotions listed on the board, or to have students review the names of some emotions before beginning the lesson.

Musical Suggestions:
Any selection from Discography.

Space Required:
It is possible to do this lesson in the regular classroom with the "seeds" sitting at their desks rather than crouching on the floor. However, students will be able to express themselves more freely and fully in an open space such as an empty classroom, gym, lunchroom, stage or outdoor area.

Time Required:
Approximately 15 minutes

Introduction:

In your lifetime you will feel many, many emotions. Certain emotions you may feel over and over again; some you may feel only rarely. Life becomes richer when we allow ourselves to experience our emotions fully and deeply instead of trying to hide them or keep them small and under control. When we really allow our emotions to fill our bodies, even the uncomfortable emotions can become like beautiful flowers in the garden of our lives.

Lesson:

(Ask students to find empty spots to stand. In the regular classroom they may remain seated in their chairs, then stand up as they "grow" into shapes.)

I'd like each of you to imagine that you are an "emotion seed." Curl yourself up very small like a seed under the ground. Let's imagine that we're all little seeds of anger. Now let your feeling of anger grow bigger and bigger until your whole body is filled with it. Let the emotion inside you make you grow into a

shape. Will the anger make your body shape straight...curved...angular...twisted? Will the anger make your shape light and floaty or strong and muscular? Will your angry shape reach wide, or be thin and narrow? Take a peek around the room and look at all the different angry shapes.

(Repeat this process with the emotions "joy" and "sadness." Continue to encourage students to really let the feeling inside them create the shapes rather than making stereotyped "happy" or "sad" shapes. Next, divide the class into two groups. Ask one group to stand against a wall while the students in the second group spread out and find empty spots in the room NOTE: In the regular classroom the second group may remain seated in their chairs.)

Those of you who are spread out in the room are "emotion seeds." Curl yourself up very small like a seed under the ground. Now, think of an emotion that your seed represents: you might be a little seed of anger, of sadness or of joy.

Emotion seeds

When the music begins, those who are standing against the wall will become gardeners dancing around the seeds. Gardeners, try many ways of moving; not just walking or running. You might skip around the seeds, turn around the seeds or float around the seeds.

(NOTE: It will be helpful for you to demonstrate the following sequence with one of the "seeds"). When you're ready, choose one seed to "water" by tapping gently on its back.

When the seed has been watered it will begin to grow into a shape, like a plant growing out of the ground. Seeds, let your emotion grow bigger and bigger until your whole body is filled with it. Let the emotion inside create your shape, like we just practiced.

When the seed has finished growing into a shape, the gardener will copy that shape. Then the gardener will curl up into a seed, and the original seed will become a gardener, dancing around until they're ready to water a new seed.

(Turn on music. Allow students three or four minutes to explore being gardeners and seeds. It is helpful to call out suggestions periodically as they move: "Have you tried slashing around the seeds? Shaking around the seeds? Sliding around the seeds? If you are a seed, what will your arms do as you grow into a shape? Your legs? Your back?" Turn

music off, and ask students to be seated for discussion.)

Growing into a sad shape

Questions for Discussion:

• How did it feel to let an emotion fill your whole body?

• Have you ever experienced an emotion that started small, then grew bigger and bigger?

• How did it feel to be the gardener who made an emotion grow? What do you think makes emotions grow in real life?

• As a gardener, when you copied someone's shape could you tell what emotion they were expressing? Did you think about their emotion, or could you actually feel it?

• What was it like to see many different emotions happening in the room at the same time?

Variations:

In the regular classroom have the "seeds" curl their upper bodies while seated in their chairs, then stand behind their chairs to create their emotion shapes. The gardener would sit in the seed's seat after copying their shape.

Once their shape has been copied, ask students to express their emotions in movement while they dance around the seeds.

Extended Activities:

Create a class mural of an "emotion garden," with each student drawing or painting a plant representing a different emotion.

Section C: The Self in Action

Who we believe ourselves to be informs the actions we take in the world. When we believe that we are powerful human beings who create our own lives, we carry out our actions with intention and confidence. When we trust our inner stability, we can act in the world with freedom and spontaneity. When we make choices with commitment, we can risk achieving our dreams.

The lessons in this section will guide students in developing a greater awareness of the kinds of choices they tend to make in their lives, and the actions that result from those choices.

Lesson 5: Spontaneity and Control

Type of Movement Activity:
Individual Improvisational Exploration
Partner Improvisational Exploration

Related Movement Concepts:
Flow (free, bound)

Materials / Preparation:
CD or tape player

Musical Suggestions:
Chappelle, Eric, "All and One" *Music for Creative Dance: Contrast and Continuum, Volume I.*

Pica, Rae "Robots and Astronauts," *Let's Move and Learn.*

Space Required:
In order for students to safely experience moving with free flow, it is suggested that this lesson be presented in a large, open space such as an empty classroom, gym, lunchroom, stage or outdoor area.

Time Required:
Approximately 15 minutes.

Introduction:

Different people like to have different amounts of control in their lives. You probably know people who are very spontaneous and free — they do whatever they want whenever they feel like it, without doing much advance planning. This type of person might even be a bit of a daredevil, or physically reckless. And perhaps you know someone who is just the opposite — who is very careful and cautious, plans ahead and takes very few risks. What about you? Are you spontaneous and free or cautious and controlled...or perhaps somewhere in between?

Lesson:

(Ask students to find an empty place to stand.)

Today we're going to experience the two types of flow our movement can have. When we move with free flow we let our bodies move without trying to control or stop them. You might feel like the wind is blowing you around the room, or like you're water flowing downhill. Staying right where you are, try moving your arms, head and back with free flow. Your neck should feel very loose and your arms will be floppy. Now let yourself travel through space as if the wind is blowing you around the room. Swirl...leap...roll...freeze. *(NOTE: If you are working in a small space, you may want to have just half of the class move at once while the other half watches, then reverse roles.)*

Now let's try the opposite kind of flow, which is called bound flow. Bound flow movement is very controlled. It can be stiff and jerky like a robot, or it can be smooth and balanced like a tightrope walker or Tai Chi master. Without traveling, try moving your body with bound flow. Try moving sharply like a robot...now smoothly like a tightrope walker. Now try traveling through the room with bound flow.

(Ask students to find a partner to work with for the next segment of the lesson.)

Let's see what it's like to copy the movements of another person as they move with free and bound flow. Please stand one behind the other as if you were going to play "follow the leader." When the music begins, the person in front will be the leader, traveling through space with free flow (or bound flow first, depending which musical selection you use. *NOTE: You may find class management easier if you begin with bound flow.)* Their partner will follow them, trying to copy their movements as closely as possible. When the music changes, the leader will switch to bound (or free) flow movement. When the music changes again, the other partner will have a chance to be the leader.

(Turn on music and allow students to complete this task. Call out movement suggestions periodically, such as: "How loose and floppy can your arms be? Can you change your level with free flow? What directions can you move in with bound flow?" At the end of the selection turn off music and ask students to be seated for discussion.)

Questions for Discussion:

• How did it feel to move with free flow?

• How did it feel to move with bound flow?

• Which type of flow felt safest to you? Why?

• Which type of flow felt most exciting? Why?

• Which type of flow did you enjoy most? Why?

• Do you think you tend to approach life in a more free flow way — "going with the flow" — or a more bound flow way — being in control?

• What are the advantages of going through life in a free, spontaneous way? The disadvantages?

• What are the advantages of going through life in a controlled way? The disadvantages?

• Was it easier to copy your partner when they moved with free flow or bound flow? Why?

• What are some situations in life where being free-flowing is helpful and appropriate?

• What are some situations where being bound and controlled is helpful and appropriate?

• Can a person choose when to be free and when to be bound?

Variations:

If you do not have access to one of the suggested musical selections you can accompany the students by using two different musical instruments — perhaps a shaker for free flow and a drum or rhythm sticks for bound flow.

Extended Activities:

Invite students to bring a piece of music from home that makes them move with either free or bound flow. Play samples of the different pieces while the class dances, and see if most people agree or disagree.

Lesson 6: Acting with Power

Type of Movement Activity:
Individual Improvisational Exploration
Partner Improvisational Exploration

Related Movement Concepts:
Weight (strong, light, active, passive)
Shape (straight, curved, angular, twisted)
Relationship (near, far, over, under, around, through)

Materials / Preparation:
None

Musical Suggestions:
No music required

Space Required:
This lesson does not require traveling through general space, and can easily be done in the aisles of a regular classroom.

Time Required:
Approximately 15 minutes

Introduction:

*Whether you realize it or not, every single one of you is a powerful person. How you choose to use your power determines what happens in your life. If you use your power actively you can accomplish just about anything. Some people, however, choose to be passive instead of active. They wait for things to happen instead of **making** things happen. They react to events instead of creating events. How do you use **your** power?*

Lesson:

(Ask students to push in their chairs and stand behind them. Several students could stand in other empty spaces in the room. If you are presenting this lesson in a large, open space, ask students to find an empty spot to stand.)

We're going to experience the different kinds of strong weight our movement can have. When we contract or tighten our muscles, we move with active weight. Try contracting your muscles and creating a body shape that is strong. Your shape can be big or small, straight or curved, high or low. Try another strong shape. Now try some strong move-ments, staying right where you are. Try pressing...pulling....punching....squeezing. How do you feel when you are using active weight?

(Allow students to respond verbally to your question. Most students will feel strong and powerful when moving with active weight.)

Now let's try the other kind of strong weight, which is called passive weight. When you're using passive weight you feel heavy and relaxed, giving in to the pull of gravity. You don't use much energy to hold yourself up. Try making a body shape with passive weight. Your arms and head might be hanging, you might lean against something or slump to the floor. Now try moving a little in self space with passive weight. Try swinging, drooping, col-lapsing. How do you feel when you are moving with passive weight?

(Allow students a minute to experience passive weight, then to respond to your question. Often students feel heavy, tired or lazy when moving with passive weight. Ask students to find a partner to work with for the next segment of the lesson.)

Now we're going to experience how active and passive weight interact together. First, I'd like you to share weight actively with your partner. Stand about two feet away from your partner, stretch both arms in front of you and press your palms against your partner's palms. You should both feel strong and be sharing the weight equally. You should not be pushing your partner over or moving them through space.

Now try sharing passive weight with your partner. Stand side by side and lean against each other. You should be using very little energy to hold your partner up.

Now let's see what happens when one partner is passive and one is active. One of you please make a shape that is very active and strong. The other partner will be passive and lean against them. Now switch roles.

Now let one person make a passive, heavy shape using very little energy. The other person will be strong and active and push against the shape. What happens? Now switch roles.

Let's end with both partners sharing weight actively one more time.

(Ask students to thank their partner, then take their seats for discussion.)

Questions for Discussion:

• What are some times in your life when you feel, or have felt, strong and powerful?

• Are there times when you feel passive — when you don't put much energy into what you're doing?

• How did it feel when you were sharing active weight with your partner? Is there a person in your life you feel equally powerful with?

• How did it feel to lean passively against your partner? Do you ever interact with someone where both of you are passive?

• When you were being active and strong, how did it feel to have the passive person lean against you? Have you ever had to be strong for someone who was being passive in your life?

• What happened when you were passive and the active person pushed against you? Why? How did it feel?

• Do you generally feel better about yourself when you are being active or when you are being passive?

• What do you think might be some of the consequences of being passive in life?

Variations:

In a large, open space students could try traveling through general space with active, passive and light weight. Active partners could try going somewhere with a passive partner leaning against them, generating a discussion on the difficulty of reaching your goals when someone is depending too heavily on you.

Extended Activities:

Give pairs of students role-play situations in which two people interact with each other actively or passively. Examples:

• An older brother is trying to get his younger sister to do his chores for him (active.) The sister doesn't want to do them, but she doesn't say no. (passive)

• One friend can't decide which TV show she wants to watch. (passive) The other friend can't make a decision either. (passive)

Have the students perform their role plays for the class, who will guess which characters are being passive and active, and how this affects the outcome of the situation.

Lesson 7: Risk and Commitment

Type of Movement Activity:
Individual Improvisational Exploration

Related Movement Concepts:
Balance (on, off)

Materials / Preparation:
drum or tambourine

Musical Suggestions:
No music required (see Variations for an alternate way of presenting the lesson using music).

Space Required:
In order for students to safely experience moving off balance it is suggested that this lesson be presented in a large, open space such as an empty classroom, gym, lunchroom, stage or outdoor area.

Time Required:
Approximately 15 minutes

Introduction:

Doing anything worthwhile and exciting in life requires some amount of risk. People who always "play it safe" stay secure, but never get to experience the satisfaction of challenging themselves to go beyond what they thought was possible. It is important to be realistic about how much risk is appropriate to take, however. Taking too much of a risk could result in getting your body or your feelings hurt. It is easier to take a risk without fear of getting hurt when you have a strong sense of what your commitments are — what you really care about in life.

Lesson:

(Ask students to find an empty spot to stand.)

We're going to use the movement concept of Balance to make discoveries about taking risks. Being on balance means that both feet are planted firmly on the ground. You should feel sturdy, stable and safe, as if nothing could knock you over. Try another shape that is on balance, maybe with two hands and two feet touching the floor. See if you can travel around the room staying on balance.

Jump...crawl...crab walk...how else can you move and be on balance?

(Allow students approximately one minute to explore moving on balance.)

Going off balance means tipping your body until you feel as if you are almost about to fall. How far can you tip without actually falling? Making your stomach muscles very strong will help keep you from falling. Try another off balance shape. Now try being off balance as you move through the room. Tip...swirl...spin...try staying on one leg as much as possible. Try letting your head pull your spine off vertical so you're never quite standing straight. Freeze.

In a moment I'll ask everyone to move around the room off balance again. This time really take a risk and see how far you can tip without falling. Remember to use your stomach muscles to hold you up. When I beat the drum (or hit the tambourine) stop wherever you are and balance on one leg until I tell you to relax. Here you go!

(Allow students to move off balance for approximately thirty seconds, then beat the drum. Let them hold their balance for

a moment or two, then ask them to stand on both feet and relax.)

What do you think made you able to hold your balance?

Certainly your muscles helped you balance — particularly your stomach and leg muscles — but there's something else that helped you that I'm going to call your "commitment to balancing." To be committed to something is to make an unbreakable promise to yourself that you're going to do it. Let's try the balancing game again, but this time right before you balance think to yourself "I will" or "I promise" and see if that makes your balance more steady. As you say that, make sure your whole body is right on top of the leg that is holding you up. You can't just balance halfway, or you will fall. Make a commitment, and put your whole self into it.

(Repeat the previous activity.)

Did making a commitment to balancing make a difference?

Let's try it again, but this time *don't* be committed. Let just part of your weight be on the leg that's holding you up; don't really give it your best try. Tell yourself "I don't care" as you hold your balance.

(Repeat the activity.)

Let's do this one more time, and this time make the strongest commitment ever. Say to yourself "I absolutely will keep my balance!"

(Repeat the activity, then ask students to be seated for discussion.)

Questions for Discussion:

• How did it feel to move on balance?

• Were there many movements you could do while staying on balance, or did you feel limited?

• How did it feel to move off balance? Was it exciting? Scary?

• Did you really take risks when you were moving off balance, or did you find yourself holding back and staying safe?

• When in your life have you really taken a risk? What happened?

• Was there ever a time in your life when you could have taken a risk but chose to play it safe? Are you glad you did?

• When you were moving off balance, did you ever find yourself taking too much of a risk? Have you ever taken too much of a risk in your life?

• Did making a commitment to holding your balance make a difference in your ability to do so? Why do you think it did or did not make a difference?

• What are you committed to in your life?

Variations:

Instead of using a drum or tambourine, you could play music while the students move off balance and stop the music to signal holding their balance on one foot. A good selection for this is "Ski Reel," *Music for Creative Dance: Contrast and Continuum, Volume II* by Eric Chappelle (see Discography).

Divide the class in half and have the students observe each other moving on balance, off balance, and with a commitment to keeping their balance.

Extended Activities:

Ask students to make a list of things they are committed to. Examples might include: taking care of a pet, being on time to a sports practice or theater rehearsal, doing homework four evenings a week.

PART TWO
DEVELOPING INTERPERSONAL SKILLS

Up to this point the lessons in this book have focused on intrapersonal awareness — on the individual's knowledge of his or her own self. In the remaining lessons we will be extending that self-awareness and examining how we, as individuals, interact with one another.

The foundation for healthy interactions with others is the ability to maintain clear personal boundaries. With these boundaries intact, we can value the differences among people without being threatened by them, and can view their actions with objectivity. Boundaries aid us in communicating clearly and listening effectively.

As our interpersonal skills grow we can begin to build a sense of trust and interdependence with others, to work cooperatively and collaboratively and to solve conflicts through negotiation and compromise. At the highest level we can serve as leaders, and can bond in solidarity with other human beings.

The lessons in this section will guide students, through movement and discussion, in developing skills for successful and fulfilling interpersonal relationships.

Section D: Maintaining Personal Boundaries
Section E: Valuing Diversity
Section F: Objectivity
Section G: Communication
Section H: Interdependence
Section I: Trust
Section J: Cooperation
Section K: Leadership

Section D: Maintaining Personal Boundaries

Setting and maintaining clear personal boundaries is at the foundation of healthy interpersonal interaction. Without clear boundaries we do not know where we end and another person begins. Setting clear boundaries makes it possible to confidently and fully be ourselves, and to allow others to be who they are.

Different individuals have different needs for personal space. Some individuals feel comfortable in very close proximity to other people, while others prefer to have a cushion of space around them. It is important to be aware of your own needs for personal space, as well as to respect the needs of others.

The lessons in this section will guide students in being aware of their personal boundaries and their need for personal space, and will provide practice in the sometimes difficult task of maintaining their individuality in the face of the pressure to conform.

Lesson 8: Personal Space

This lesson is based on a Creative Dance exploration created by Anne Green Gilbert

Type of Movement Activity:
Group Improvisational Exploration

Related Movement Concepts:
Place (self space, general space)
Size (big, medium, little)
Relationships (near, far, over, under, around, through)

Materials / Preparation:
CD or tape player (optional)

Musical Suggestions:
Chappelle, Eric, "All and One," *Music for Creative Dance, Contrast and Continuum,*

Volume I (see Discography), or any selection with clearly defined sections of 20 to 30 seconds each.

This lesson can also be presented without music.

Space Required:
Because this lesson deals explicitly with large and small spaces, it needs to be presented in a large, open space such as an empty classroom, gym, lunchroom, stage or outdoor area.

Time Required:
Approximately 15 minutes

Introduction:

Each of us has an invisible personal space surrounding our body, which follows us everywhere we go. This space is called our kinesphere, from two Latin words meaning "body sphere" or "body circle." Our personal space can grow or shrink depending on the size of the area we're in, who we are with and how we feel.

Lesson:

(Ask students to find an empty spot to stand.)

Let's begin by exploring our kinespheres. Imagine you have a huge sphere all around your body, as if you're enclosed in a bubble. Use your hands to feel the bubble all around you — in front of you, behind you, to both sides, above your head and below your feet. Now stretch as wide as you can and make your kinesphere grow or expand. Now shrink your body and let your kinesphere contract around you.

Now try walking around the room, imagining the kinespheres surrounding everyone's bodies. As you walk past someone try to give them plenty of space so your kinesphere doesn't touch theirs. Freeze.

When I turn on the music, please imagine that you're in a big open space — maybe a huge meadow or a football field. Move all around, stretching your body and kinesphere as far as you can.

When the music changes, we'll pretend the space has shrunk in half, and we can only move on this side of the room. (*Indicate clearly where the imaginary boundary will be*). Your movements will have to become smaller to fit in just half of the room.

The next time the music changes the space will shrink in half again, and we'll only move in this quarter of the room. (*Indicate the boundaries clearly.*) See what happens to the size of your kinesphere when you're moving in this small space.

On the next musical change we'll all crowd together as closely as we can in this corner of the room, trying to move around each other. Our kinespheres will have to be tiny!

Last of all, we'll spread out and move in the whole big space again.

(Turn music on and guide students in completing the described activity. Remind them of the new boundaries at each musical change, and suggest move-ments for them to try: "Have you tried skipping or leaping in the big space? Can you move backwards or sideways in this half of the room? How far can your arms stretch when you're only moving in one quarter of the room? Is it possible to change level in this tiny corner?"

Turn music off and ask students to be seated for discussion.

NOTE: You may do this activity without music, signaling the changes with a drum or other instrument. However, you will find that music will help the students feel less inhibited, especially in doing larger movements.)

Questions for Discussion:

- How did it feel to move in the whole big space? Did you feel free? Excited? Shy?

- How did you feel when the space started shrinking? What did you notice about your movements?

- What was it like to dance in the tiny corner? Did you like it? Did it feel uncomfortable?

- How did you feel when you could move in the big space again after being cramped in the corner?

- Do you feel most comfortable being very far from other people, very close to other people, or somewhere in between?

- What are some of the advantages of being far from other people? What are some of the disadvantages?

- What are some of the advantages of being very close to other people? What are some of the disadvantages?

- Do you have more choices of how to move when you're very close to people, or very far?

• Do all people feel comfortable with the same amount of space around them? Give some examples from life showing that people enjoy having different amounts of personal space.

Variations:

In presenting this lesson you could use the imagery of a rural area that becomes more and more built up and crowded until it is a densely populated city.

Extended Activities:

Ask students to collect photographs from magazines showing people with varied amounts of space around them: crowded cities, a lone backpacker, people dancing together, etc. Create a class "Personal Space" collage.

Lesson 9: Personal Space Conversations

Type of Movement Activity:
Partner Improvisational Exploration

Related Movement Concepts:
Place (self space, general space)
Size (big, medium, little)
Relationships (near, far, over, under, around, through)

Materials / Preparation:
CD player or tape deck (optional)

Musical Suggestions:
Any selection from Discography

Space Required:
This lesson can be adjusted to fit the size of the space you are working in. Optimally, students would be able to begin the activity standing about six feet away from a partner.

Time Required:
Approximately 15 minutes

Introduction:

As you know, different people are comfortable with different amounts of personal space around them. Have you ever noticed that some people come very close when they talk to you, while other people stand farther away? Maybe you've experienced having someone stand so close that you felt a little uncomfortable. The other person was perfectly comfortable, but you needed more personal space.

Personal space varies not only from person to person, but from culture to culture. In Italy, for example, many people come very close to the person they are conversing with while in Japan people tend to stand farther away.

Lesson:

(Ask students to find a partner, then stand facing their partner with about six feet of space between them. NOTE: You

may need to adjust the amount of space between the partners to fit the size of the room you are working in. Another option for presenting this lesson in a small space is to have only half of the students do the activity while the other half watches, then reverse roles.)

Today you are going to have a conversation with your partner — but instead of using words you'll be speaking with movement. Here's how it works: one of you will start the conversation by doing a few movements in self space (without traveling). This person might simply move one body part for a few seconds — maybe they'll nod their head a few times, or swing their arms. Or they might choose to do several movements with their whole body. It's as if they're saying a short sentence such as "How are you today?" When they're done with their turn, they freeze.

Then it's the other partner's turn to move. They might try to imagine what their friend was saying, and use their body to answer back. Again, they will keep it short and freeze when their turn is done.

Movement conversation

(It will be helpful to demonstrate this sequence of "speaking" back and forth several times with a student to make sure everyone is clear about what to do.)

You will speak with your body back and forth to each other, like a real conversation. When I turn the music off (*or give another signal if you are not using music*), you and your partner will take one giant step closer to each other, then begin your conversation again. You'll move a step closer each time the music stops until your are only an inch or two away from each other.

(Ask pairs to choose one person to start the conversation, then turn on the music or signal them to begin. It will be helpful to give suggestions aloud as they "converse" such as: "Try moving your arms... your head...your legs. Try some big movements...some tiny movements. You might slash...poke...dab...flick."

As indicated above, stop the conversations periodically and cue the partners to take a step closer together. Repeat the procedure until they are having a conversation only an inch or two away from each other. Turn music off or signal students to freeze, then ask them to be seated for discussion.)

Questions for Discussion:

• How did it feel to be very far away from your partner during your conversation? What did you notice about your movements?

• How did you feel when I asked you to move closer to your partner? Did your movements change?

• What was it like to have a conversation when you were just an inch or two away from your partner?

• At what distance from your partner did you feel most comfortable? Why?

• Are there any situations in life when you might find yourself far away from someone you are speaking to? How would you adjust?

• When might you find yourself very close to a person you are speaking to? How would you adjust?

• How might you know that you are standing too close to another person, and that they need more personal space?

• What can you do if you feel like someone is too close to you, and you need more personal space?

Variations:

If your students appear self-conscious about doing this activity, you might try doing it with the class divided into two large groups. The groups would take turns moving, then take a step closer to each other at the given signal.

Extended Activities:

Ask students to be aware of their personal space over the next few days, and to be ready to share an incident where they either had to speak to someone at a great distance (i.e.: across the playground) or were so close to another person that they felt uncomfortable. The students should share, in either situation, what they did to adjust to the distance or closeness.

Lesson 10: Keeping Your Own Rhythm

Type of Movement Activity:
Small Group Improvisational Exploration

Related Movement Concepts:
Rhythm (pulse, breath)
Relationship (near, far, over, under, around, through)

Materials / Preparation:
Hand drum or other percussion instrument

Space Required:
As this lesson does not require traveling through general space, it could be presented in the aisles and open areas of the regular classroom. However, the lesson will be most successful in a large, open area such as an empty classroom, gym, lunchroom, stage or outdoor area.

Time Required:
Approximately 15 minutes

Introduction:

One of the biggest challenges in keeping your personal boundaries strong is to do what feels right for you, even when the people around you are doing something different.

Lesson:

(Ask students to find an empty place to stand.)

I'm going to play a 4/4 marching rhythm on the drum. See if you can march in self space (without traveling) to this beat.

(Play a medium tempo marching rhythm, allowing students to march in self space for 15 or 20 seconds.)

Let's try it again, and see if you can add a sharp slashing movement with your arms. Alternate right and left arms, slashing on each beat as you march.

(Repeat the marching rhythm, allowing students to march and slash in self space for 15 or 20 seconds.)

Now I'm going to play a completely different rhythm called a ³/₄ or waltz rhythm. See if you can sway and swing your arms from side to side on the first beat of each measure.

(Play a medium tempo ³/₄ rhythm, allowing students to swing their arms in self space for 15 to 20 seconds. Although you will play all three beats, make sure they swing only on count one of each measure: swing 2 3, swing 2 3, etc.

Ask students to get into groups of four.)

Now I'm going to play a steady beat on the drum. Three people in each group will march and slash and one person will swing. The marchers will be counting 1 2 3 4, 1 2 3 4 in their heads, while the person swinging thinks 1 2 3, 1 2 3. This is very tricky, so just do your best and notice what it's like being a marcher or the swinger. Stay close to your group in self space, and continue until I stop playing.

(Ask students to choose one person in each group to swing. Play a steady beat at a medium tempo without accenting any beats. Continue for about thirty seconds, then stop. Repeat the activity until every person in each group has had a chance to be the one who swings. Be aware that this is a difficult task, and that the groups will have varying amounts of success. The point is to experience attempting the activity, not doing it perfectly. Ask the students to be seated for discussion.)

Questions for Discussion:

- Did you find it easier to march and slash or to swing on the drumbeats?

- Why was it difficult to swing when everyone else in your group was slashing?

- What did you have to do in order to keep your own rhythm when you were swinging?

- How did it feel to be the one who was doing something different from the rest of the group? Did you feel left out? Proud? Frustrated?

- How did it feel to be in the marching group? When you were in that group, how did you feel about the person who was swinging?

- Has there ever been a time in your life when you've chosen not to "follow the crowd," but to do something different from the people around you? What happened? How did you feel?

- In what situations do you think it might be important to do something different from what the people around you are doing?

Variations:

If you have a class that is experienced with movement and rhythm, ask the groups of four to create their own movement to the 4/4 beat. Three students would do the group movement in unison, while one improvised a contrasting movement.

Start by having three students march and one student in each group swing, then one by one have the marchers join the swinger till all four are swinging. This could lead to a discussion on the impact a person can make on others when they "follow the beat of a different drummer."

Extended Activities:

Ask students to write a short story describing a situation where someone decides not to "follow the crowd."

Section E: Valuing Diversity

As a child begins to develop beyond the egocentric stage where he views himself as the center of the universe with others being merely an extension of his own consciousness, he can start to look outside his own boundaries and notice the similarities and differences between himself and other people. This child can begin to appreciate the amazing diversity in physical characteristics, ethnic origin and culture that exists among human beings. At a more subtle level, he can begin to distinguish the diversity of choices that people can make in any given situation, and to see value in those choices, even if they might be different from his own.

The following lesson gives an illustration, in movement, of the diversity of responses that are possible to a single problem.

Lesson 11: Diverse Choices

Type of Movement Activity:
Individual Improvisational Exploration
Individual Choreography

Related Movement Concepts:
All concepts (see Movement Concepts chart)

Materials / Preparation:
The following words listed on a chalkboard or piece of butcher paper:

     walk   turn
     jump   skip
        freeze

CD player or tape deck

Musical Suggestions:
Any selection from Discography

Space Required:
This lesson requires adequate space for the entire class to travel through general space at once. An empty classroom, gym, lunchroom, stage or outdoor area are suggested.

Time Required:
Approximately 15 minutes

Introduction:

Although there are many ways in which most people are similar, there are also significant differences between people. People look different, speak differently and come from different cultural and family backgrounds. People also think and view the world differently from one another and, because of this, make a wide variety of choices in their lives. One word for these differences between people is "diversity." When we accept and value diversity we can appreciate many kinds of people, even if the choices they make are very different from our own.

Lesson:

(Ask students to find an empty spot to stand.)

On the board I've written five words describing movements that I'm sure are very familiar to you. Let's read the words together.

Even though these movements are quite common, each one of them can be performed in an almost infinite number of ways. Let's experiment with some of the many ways it is possible to do each of these movements.

(Turn on music.)

Let's start with the movement "walk." Begin walking as you usually do. Now find a way to change your walk. Could you make it slower? Faster? Could you add arm movements to your walk? Head movements? Try walking in a different direction, like backwards or sideways. Try walking in straight lines…circles…zigzags. Is it possible to walk on a different level?

(Continue as above with each of the other four words. For the word "freeze" encourage students to freeze in high shapes, low shapes, big shapes, little shapes, straight shapes, curved shapes, etc. It will be helpful to both you and the students to have a list of the Movement Concepts posted to refer to during this lesson. Turn music off.)

Now that you've experimented with many different ways to do each movement, I'd like you to make a choice about how you'd like to do each one. I'll call out the words again, and this time be sure you decide exactly how you are going to do each word as I call it. Try to remember the choices you make, because in a moment you'll be showing your movements to the rest of the class.

(Turn on music. Say all five words again, allowing approximately 10 seconds between each word for students to move. If it looks like all students have made clear choices of how to perform each word, turn music off. Or, you may want to have them practice and remember their choices one more time.

Ask half of the class to be seated.)

Now I'm going to call out the five words again and let the students who are standing show you their choices. If you are watching, notice any movement choices that really surprise you; that you might never have thought of.

(Turn on music. Call the five words again, allowing 10 seconds between each word for students to show their choices. Turn music off. Repeat with the other half of the class performing.)

Questions for Discussion:

• Which movement choices really stood out for you or caught your eye. Why?

• Was there ever a time when everyone was moving in exactly the same way?

• What was it like to see so many ways of interpreting the same word?

• Were any of the choices right or wrong?

• What do you think might cause certain people to prefer particular choices?

• Were you more drawn to watching choices that were similar to your own, or very different from your own?

• Now that you've seen some choices made by other people, do you think you might change your own choices if we were to do this again?

• What are some advantages of diversity? Some disadvantages?

Variations:

You could have each half of the class repeat this activity to see if they were impacted by the alternative choices they saw.

Extended Activities:

For the next week, focus students' attention on a different aspect of diversity each day: ethnic diversity, diversity in family background, diverse talents, diverse interests, etc. You could keep the focus on diversity among students in the class or extend it to embrace world-wide diversity.

Section F: Objectivity

In viewing an action or event or observing the behavior of another person, it is human nature to create an interpretation of what one has just seen. The problem with such interpretations is that they tend to be a product of the observer's past experiences and expectations, and may have very little to do with the reality of the event or the behavior being observed.

Cultivating objectivity — the ability to observe an event or action without adding one's own interpretation — allows us to be present with other people. It gives us a chance to truly be open to others instead of deciding in advance who they are and what their actions mean.

The following lesson gives students an opportunity to experience and discuss how their interpretations color their observations, and to practice observing an event objectively.

Lesson 12: Interpretations

Type of Movement Activity:
Individual Improvisational Exploration
Small Group Choreography

Related Movement Concepts:
Directions (forward, backwards, left, right, up, down)
Relationship (near, far, over, under, around, through, together, apart)

Materials / Preparation:
3x5 cards, each with one of the following six words written on it (you will need one set of six cards for each group of four or five students):

advance	retreat
open	close
rise	sink

The same six words should be listed on the chalkboard or a piece of butcher paper.

Musical Suggestions:
Any selection from Discography

Space Required:
This lesson requires adequate space for groups of students to work simultaneously in creating movement studies. Presenting the entire lesson in a large, open space such as an empty classroom, gym, lunchroom, stage or outdoor area would be optimal. Alternatively, present the improvisational portion of the lesson in the regular classroom and send groups of students to different areas of the classroom to choreograph. (You may want to send one or two groups into a hallway if that is feasible.)

Time Required:
Approximately 30 minutes

Introduction:

Who can tell us what it means to "interpret" an event or action? That's right — an interpretation is an idea you make up to explain what something means or why it happens. Sometimes our interpretations are correct, but sometimes they're not. Having a false interpretation of something keeps us from seeing that event or action as it really is.

Lesson:

(Ask students to find an empty spot to stand.)

I've written six words on the board which relate to the movement concept of Directions — whether we're traveling forward, backward, sideways or up and down.

Let's start with the word advance, which means to go forward. First, try letting just one body part advance — maybe your arm. Now try advancing your whole body slowly through space. When you advance, the front of your body is pulling you. Turn and face a different wall, and advance slowly toward it. Now turn to face a different wall and advance toward it quickly.

The word retreat means to pull back or move backward. Try letting your arm retreat behind you. Now retreat your whole body slowly, moving backward as if the back of your body is being pulled. Turn to face another wall and try retreating with big steps…how about little steps.

Let's put the movements "open" and "close" together. Try opening one side of your body by reaching your arm sideways. Now close that side by folding your arm across your body. Try that on the other side. Now try opening and closing both sides at once:

stretch wide, then curl inward. Try opening one side of your body and letting it pull you sideways through space. Let the other side open and pull you in the opposite direction.

To rise means to move upward and to sink means to move downward. Let your arm rise, then sink. Let your whole body rise up on tiptoe, then sink gently to the floor.

(Ask students to be seated while you give directions for the choreography project.)

In a moment I'll divide you into groups of four or five. Each group will get six cards, each with one of the six direction words on it. Your first job with your group will be to put the six cards in an order that you all agree on.

(You may want to model this process using six cards and asking various students to raise their hands to suggest which card should go first, last, etc. Be sure to model resolving disagreements through negotiation and compromise.)

After you've decided on an order for your six words, decide as a group how you will perform each word. Be sure to create relationships with each other. For example, maybe you'll all stand in a straight line and advance toward the audience. Or maybe you'll stand in a circle and advance toward each other. Think about whether you'll be near or far from each other as you do a movement, or whether you'll move together or apart. Be sure your movement study has a clear beginning and end. Practice it several times so you'll be able to remember it.

(With an inexperienced group you may want to begin by having the whole class choreograph a study together before dividing into groups. Divide students

into groups of four or five, giving each group the six word cards. Circulate among the groups as they work, providing assistance and suggestions as needed.

When all groups have finished creating their studies, allow each group to perform their study for the class with music. After each performance ask the audience members the following questions):

How would you interpret what you just saw? What do you think the study was about? What did it mean? What would be a good title for the study?

Now, can you describe the study without creating an interpretation? How would you describe it to a person who couldn't see? Try describing only what the performers were actually doing, for example: "They all stood in a circle and walked toward each other."

(Repeat this process after each performance. At the conclusion of the entire activity, discuss the following):

Questions for Discussion:

• Was it easier for you to create an interpretation of what the studies were about, or to describe them without interpretation?

• How many different interpretations were there for each study?

• Where do you think interpretations come from?

• Can you think of a situation in your life when you created an interpretation and it ended up being false? What happened?

• What are some situations in which it would be important to simply describe what happened rather than interpreting actions?

Variations:

It is possible to present this lesson using virtually any movement words. Try using the Basic Effort Action words (see Chapter 3) or any words from the listing of Locomotor and Non-Locomotor Movements.

After hearing the audience's interpretations, allow the performers to choose one and revise their study to reflect that interpretation.

Extended Activities:

Have students look at works of abstract art and interpret what they see. Then challenge them to describe the works objectively in terms of color, shape, etc.

Section G: Communication

Communication is at the foundation of effective interpersonal relationships. Communication facilitates us as human beings in connecting with each other, sharing our experiences and asking for what we need.

Although we tend to think of communication as taking place predominantly through the spoken or written word, it also consists of several other elements including facial expression, body posture and movement. When these elements match our words, our communication comes across as an integrated whole. When one of these elements is at odds with our words, our communication is unclear. When our actions are contradictory to our spoken communication, we give our listeners a mixed message.

Just as important as the active skill of communicating clearly is the skill of listening receptively. Too often we don't really take in what another person is communicating to us, but instead are planning what we will say in reply. The best communication is a two-way process of speaking, listening, reflecting and questioning.

The lessons in this section will guide students in experiencing, through movement, the skills required for clear communication and effective listening.

Lesson 13: Mixed Messages

Type of Movement Activity:
Individual Improvisational Exploration

Related Movement Concepts:
Weight (strong, light)
Energy (smooth, sharp)

Materials / Preparation:
None

Musical Suggestions:
No music required

Space Required:
This lesson requires very little space and can easily be presented in the regular classroom with students standing behind their chairs. It would also be exciting to present in a large, open space.

Time Required:
Approximately 10 minutes

Introduction:

When we communicate with other people we use not only our voices and words, but our bodies and actions as well. When our actions don't match what we're saying we're giving the person listening to us a "mixed message." When our words and actions match, our communication comes across as truthful and clear.

Lesson:

(Ask students to stand behind their chairs, or in an empty spot in the room.)

Today we'll work with two movements that feel almost the opposite of each other: floating and punching. Let's start with the word "float." Right where you are, without traveling, try some floating movements with your body. Floating is very light and smooth. Think of how a cloud moves as it floats across the sky. Try floating your arms…your legs…your head. Maybe you'll balance or turn as you float.

Keep floating, and as you move softly say the word "float" over and over.

Now let's try the word "punch." Be sure you're standing far enough away from your neighbor that you'll only punch the air. Begin by punching with your arms. A punch is strong and quick, as if you're thrusting your fist through something. Now try punching with a foot…your head.

Keep punching, and as you move say the word "punch" over and over in a powerful voice.

Now we'll try something that might feel a little strange: see if you can float with your body, but say the word punch with your voice.

(Allow students approximately 10 seconds to experiment with this.)

Now try the opposite: see if you can punch while you say the word "float."

(Allow students approximately 10 seconds to experiment with this, then ask half the class to take their seats while the other half remains standing.)

Let's watch each other now. I'd like the people who are standing to float their bodies as they say the word "float."

Now I'd like them to continue floating, but to say the word "punch."

Now please punch as you say "punch"…

…and punch as you say "float."

(Allow this group approximately 10 seconds for each one of the preceding tasks, then repeat with the other half of the class.)

Questions for Discussion:

- When you were moving, how did it feel to say one thing and do another?
- When you were watching, how did it feel to see people saying one thing and doing another?
- Did you feel differently when their words matched their actions?
- Did you find yourself paying more attention to their words or their actions? Why?
- Have you ever been with someone who said one thing and did another? What happened? How did you feel?

Variations:

For a more intimate experience, have students watch one another do this activity in pairs, then ask them to discuss the preceding questions with their partners.

Extended Activities:

Give each student a card with a simple "I" statement on it such as:

- I would never take something that isn't mine.
- I never eat sweets.
- I'm always kind to other people.

Each student would have an opportunity to demonstrate saying the statement on the card while pantomiming an action that is contradictory to their words.

Lesson 14: Listening

Type of Movement Activity:
Partner Improvisational Exploration

Related Movement Concepts:
Place (self space, general space)
Body Parts (head, arms, elbows, legs, etc.)

Materials / Preparation:
Tape deck or CD player (optional)

Musical Suggestions:
Any selection from Discography

This lesson can also be presented without music.

Space Required:
This lesson does not require traveling through space, and could easily be presented in the regular classroom.

Time Required:
Approximately 10 minutes

Introduction:

Often when we think of communication we focus our attention on the person who is speaking. The listener, however, has an equally important job. It requires a great deal of openness and concentration to accurately receive the message the speaker is trying to get across. Being a good listener is a valuable skill that requires practice.

Lesson:

(Ask students to stand facing a partner, about two feet away from each other. NOTE: If your class has already completed Lesson 9: Personal Space Conversations and/or has had prior experience with movement conversations, you may choose to omit these preliminary instructions.)

Today you're going to have a conversation with your partner using movement instead of words. One of you will start the conversation by doing a few movements in self space; without traveling. This person might move just one body part for a few seconds — maybe they'll nod their head a few times, or swing their arms. Or they might move their whole body for a few seconds. It's as if they're saying a short sentence like "How are you today?" When they're done with their turn, they freeze.

Then it's the other partner's turn to speak. They might try to imagine what the first person was saying, then use their body to answer back. Again, they'll keep it short and freeze when their turn is done.

(It will be helpful to demonstrate this sequence several times with a student.)

As you speak back and forth with each other using your body, I'd like you to imagine that you're trying to impress each other with what an amazing story your body is telling. Try to prove to each other how smart and creative you are. If your partner does an interesting movement, try to top him or her by doing a movement that is even *more* interesting.

(Ask students to choose one person in each pair to begin the conversation, then turn on the music or signal them to begin. It is helpful to give suggestions as they "converse": "Try moving your arms...your head...your legs. Try some big movements...some tiny movements. You might slash...poke...dab...flick." Allow students to continue "conversing" in this way for one to two minutes, then turn music off or signal them to freeze.)

I'd like you to continue your movement conversations, but to change one thing: This time the person who is not moving will have to watch their partner very carefully because they'll need to begin their reply by repeating one of the movements they just saw their partner do. This time the emphasis is not on trying to impress your partner, but on making sure you are able to repeat at least one of their movements exactly. Once you've copied one of their movements you can add a few movements of your own, but be sure to make

them simple and clear so your partner will also be able to copy you.

(Turn on music. Allow students one to two minutes to "converse" in this new way, then turn music off and ask students to be seated for discussion.)

Questions for Discussion:

• Did the two ways of having a conversation feel different to you? What made them different?

• What was it like to know that you were going to have to repeat one of you partner's movements? How did that change the way you watched your partner?

• How did you feel when you knew that your partner was watching you carefully so that he or she would be able to copy you?

• Have you ever had a conversation with someone in which both of you were trying to impress each other rather than really communicating and listening? What happened? How did it feel?

• Is there anyone in your life who is a really good listener? How can you tell they are listening to you?

• If you had to write a list of things that make a good listener, what would be on your list?

Variations:

You could present this lesson with the entire class standing in a circle. One person would begin the conversation by moving for a few seconds. The next person would reply, and so on around the circle. In the second segment of the activity the person moving would always have to repeat at least one movement done by the previous person before adding movements of their own.

Extended Activities:

Have students practice listening to each other in verbal conversations. The person replying must repeat or "reflect" something said by the speaker before adding a comment of their own. For example:

- Speaker #1: I really hope it's sunny this weekend so I can go on a picnic with my family.

- Speaker #2: It sounds like you're really excited about having a picnic this weekend. I'm planning to play baseball with some friends.

Lesson 15: Asking Questions

Type of Movement Activity:
Partner Shapes

Related Movement Concepts:
Shapes (straight, curved, angular, twisted, wide, narrow)

Materials / Preparation:
None

Musical Suggestions:
No music required

Space Required:
This lesson does not require traveling through space and could easily be presented in the regular classroom.

Time Required:
Approximately 15 minutes

Introduction:

We know that in communication it is important for the speaker to deliver their message clearly and for the listener to listen attentively. However, no matter how clear the speaker or attentive the listener, sometimes the message is not received accurately. As a listener, one of the best ways to make sure you are receiving a message accurately is to ask questions.

Lesson:

(Ask students to stand behind their chairs.)

We're going to begin today by experimenting with some of the different shapes our bodies can make. First let's try making body shapes that are very straight. In a straight shape all your body parts should be stretched, with nothing bent. Try another straight shape. You could be straight and wide or straight and narrow.

Now curve your body parts to create a curved, rounded shape. Curve your arms, your legs, your back. Make sure all your body parts are curved, with no sharp angles. Try a big curved shape…a small curved shape.

Now bend your joints to create an angular shape. Bend your elbows and knees, flex your feet and ankles. Your shape should look as if it has sharp points on it. Try a balancing angular shape.

Last of all try creating a twisted shape with your body. You might twist at the waist like a wet towel being wrung dry, or you might tangle your body parts like a pretzel or a knot. Try several different twisted shapes.

Now try making a shape that combines straight, curved, angular and twisted. Perhaps one arm will be straight, the other arm curved, a leg angular and your waist twisted.

(Ask students to find a partner to work with. You may want to model the next sequence of directions using yourself and a student before having the class work on their own.)

Designate one partner to be the speaker and one to be the listener, then stand back to back so you can't see each other. The speaker will make a shape with their body, then describe the shape to the listener who will try to reproduce it according to the description, without being able to see the shape. Speaker, tell the listener as clearly as you can where their arms should go, what their legs and back should look like, if they should be straight or curved, angular or twisted, wide or narrow, big or small. As the shape is being described the listener will do their best to follow the speaker's directions. Then the speaker will turn around and see how accurately the listener was able to reproduce the shape. Then reverse the roles, and give the listener a chance to be the speaker.

(Allow students several minutes to complete this task. Make sure both partners have had an opportunity to experience each role before moving on to the next segment of the lesson.)

Now we'll try the same thing again, but this time the listener can ask questions. For example, if the speaker says "Your arm should be straight," the listener might ask "Should it be high or low?" Ask as many questions as you need to in order to be sure you are making the shape correctly. When you are finished, the speaker will look at the shape to see how accurately it was reproduced this time. Then

switch roles again so you both have a chance to be both the listener and the speaker.

(Allow students several minutes to complete this task. After each student has had a turn to be both the speaker and the listener, ask students to be seated for discussion.)

Questions for Discussion:

• When the listeners were not allowed to ask questions, how accurately did they reproduce the speakers' shapes?

• Did the accuracy of the shapes increase when the listeners were allowed to ask questions?

• As a speaker, did it help you to guide your listener in reproducing your shape when they were able to ask you questions?

• Did you find it uncomfortable at all to ask questions?

• What are some things that stop you from asking questions at school? At home?

• Do you ever wish that someone in your life would ask you more questions? Who and why?

Variations:

Instead of doing this activity in partners, it could be done in groups of three or four with one person being the speaker and the others being listeners. The speaker would be able to see how each of the listeners interpreted his or her directions differently.

Extended Activities:

Ask students to make a point of asking questions when they are unclear about something at school or at home. Encourage them to keep a record for a week of situations in which they asked questions and what the results were.

Section H: Interdependence

As much as our current society values independence and autonomy, it is important to acknowledge that human beings are naturally interrelated and interdependent. It is valuable to be able to choose when you are willing to give and receive support from others, and when it is truly appropriate to "stand on your own two feet."

As human beings, we are profoundly impacted by our interactions with others. Our relationships with other people in many ways shape both who we are and how we see ourselves. It takes skill and practice to negotiate the constantly changing landscape of our personal connections.

In today's world it is very easy to feel isolated and disconnected from other people, and to therefore assume that our actions do not affect others. One of the most valuable insights we can provide for children is the knowledge that their actions make an impact on the world — that who they are and what they do truly does make a difference.

The lessons in this section will guide students in exploring and experiencing, through movement, the connection between independence and interdependence, the role of change in human relationships and the possibility that their actions can make a profound impact on others.

Lesson 16:
Independence—Interdependence

Type of Movement Activity:
Partner Shapes
Group Improvisational Exploration

Related Movement Concepts:
Weight (strong, light)
Balance (on, off)
Relationship (near, far, over, under, around, through, together, apart)

Materials / Preparation:
CD player or tape deck

Musical Suggestions:
Any selection from Discography

Space Required:
Although it is possible to present this lesson in a regular classroom with students making shapes and moving between and around desks, it would be more successfully presented in a large, open space such as an empty classroom, gym, lunchroom, stage or outdoor area.

Time Required:
Approximately 15 minutes

Introduction:

Who can tell me what it means to be "independent? That's right, it means being able to take care of yourself without having to depend on someone else. Although it is important to have a sense of independence, human beings are more often interdependent — they give support to and receive support from one another. Being interdependent is a sign of strength rather than weakness, because it means that you are able to stand on your own, but are choosing to share support with another.

Lesson:

(Ask students to find a partner.)

We'll begin by seeing what it's like to "share weight" with a partner. *(NOTE: Students who have already experienced Lesson 6: Acting with Power will be familiar with the concept of sharing weight.)*

Stand facing your partner, about two feet away from each other. Hold both arms straight in front of you, press your palms together and lean into one another. You should both be pressing equally, with neither person pushing the other over. If you are truly sharing weight, you should be perfectly balanced against each other, and will not travel at all.

Now let's try a side-to-side weight sharing shape. Turn so that both you and your partner are facing the same direction with your sides toward each other. Stretch one arm sideways toward your partner and press palms together as you lean into one another sideways. It might feel like you're leaning against a wall. Again, make sure you're holding your partner up just as much as they're supporting you.

(Divide the class into thirds. Ask the first group to find a spot in the room to stand. The students in the second group will become their partners, finding one person in the first group to make a weight sharing shape with. The students in the third group should remain standing against a wall.)

When the music begins, everyone who is standing against the wall will start moving around the weight-sharing shapes. Try many different ways of moving, not just walking or running. When you are ready, you will come up to a weight sharing shape and tap one of the partners lightly. The tap will be that person's signal to disconnect from their partner and move away. Once they have left, give their partner a moment to stand alone, then join them in a new weight sharing shape. The person who left will keep moving around the shapes until they are ready to tap someone else. Continue in this way until I turn off the music.

(Allow students approximately three minutes to explore the activity just described. Guide them in moving creatively by calling out suggestions as they move, for example: "Have you tried moving backward around the shapes? Try changing your speed as you move. What are some ways you could move your arms as you travel around the shapes?" After about three minutes, turn the music off and ask students to be seated for discussion.)

Questions for Discussion:

• How did it feel to share weight with someone?

- Did it feel the same to share weight with each person you worked with? What did you have to do to adapt to each new partner?

- Describe what happened when you were sharing weight and your partner was tapped. How did you feel? What did you have to do in order to be able to stand by yourself without falling over?

- Did you ever find that you were leaning too heavily on someone? What happened when that person got tapped?

- Did you feel most comfortable when you were sharing weight, or when you were standing alone? Why?

- Are there any situations in your life in which you feel you give and receive support equally with someone? How does that feel? What would it be like if that person were no longer there?

- Is there anyone you feel you depend on too much? What would it be like if that person were no longer there?

- What are some situations in which you prefer to be completely independent, and do everything by yourself?

- What are some situations in which you prefer to share support with other people?

- What are some advantages of independence? Some disadvantages?

- What are some advantages of interdependence? Some disadvantages?

Variations:

Have more experienced students explore sharing weight between other body parts — backs, shoulders, feet, hips. Partners might try weight sharing shapes on different levels, or on opposite levels from each other.

Extended Activities:

Ask students to choose two photographs from magazines; one illustrating independence, one showing interdependence. Be sure to point out that the "independence" photograph doesn't necessarily have to be of just one person. A picture of ten people walking down a street might illustrate independence if each person were walking alone, not relating to the others.

Lesson 17: Changing Relationships

Type of Movement Activity:
Partner Shapes
Group Improvisational Exploration

Related Movement Concepts:
Shapes (straight, curved, angular, twisted)
Relationships (near, far, over, under, around, through)

Materials / Preparation:
CD player or tape deck

Musical Suggestions:
Any selection from Discography

Space Required:
Although it is possible to present this lesson in a regular classroom with students creating shapes and moving between and around desks, it would optimally take place in a large, open space such as an empty classroom, gym, lunchroom, stage or outdoor area.

Time Required:
Approximately 15 minutes

Introduction:

For most people, experiencing relationships with other human beings is probably the most important and satisfying part of life. Through relating to others we learn about ourselves. Although some people, such as members of our family, may be in relationship with us throughout our entire lives, much of life is composed of changing relationships. We meet new people that we care about, and perhaps lose contact with people we were once close to. Even our relationships to the people that remain in our lives for many years will change, because people themselves are constantly changing.

Lesson:

(Ask students to find a partner to work with.)

In movement, we can use the words near, far, over, under, around, through, between and on to create shapes in relationship to a partner. As I say each word, try creating a shape with your partner which shows what that word means.

Near...how close to each other can you be in your shape?

Far...can you stay connected to your partner, but stretch some body parts far away?

Over...will one body part reach over another? Could one person make a bridge over the other?

Under...could you both imagine that you're underneath something?

Around...try curving your arm around your partner or twisting your bodies around each other.

Through...find an empty space in your partner's shape and reach an arm, leg or head through it.

Aroung and through

Between...could you reach a body part between your partner's knees or elbows?

On...try a shape with one part of your body resting on your partner.

(Divide the class in half. Ask one half of the students to find an empty spot in the room and make an interesting shape with their bodies. The other students should remain standing against a wall. It will be helpful to demonstrate the following directions with one of the students.)

When I turn on the music, those of you who are against a wall will begin to move around the shapes. Try many different ways of moving: skipping, floating, jumping, moving slowly, moving quickly, moving strongly, moving lightly. When you're ready, come to one of the shapes and create your own shape in relationship to it. Think about some of the words you just learned to help give you ideas: You might make a shape that is over or under the original shape, that reaches around it or pokes through one of its empty spaces. When the original person feels that you have created a clear relationship, he or she will disconnect from the shape as carefully as possible and begin moving around the room. The person who just created the relationship will hold their position until someone else comes to join them. The person who left will keep moving until they find a new shape to create a relationship with. Continue in this way until I turn off the music.

(Turn on music and allow students approximately three minutes to explore the activity described above. Turn music off and ask students to be seated for discussion.)

Questions for Discussion:

- When you were a mover, how did you decide what type of relationship to create with one of the shapes?

- Were some shapes easier to create a relationship with than others? Which type of shape, and why?

- How did it feel when someone created a relationship with your shape? Were you ever surprised by the relationship that was created?

- Was it easy or difficult to disconnect from your partner? Which types of shapes were most difficult to disconnect from?

- How did it feel when your partner disconnected from you? Were you ever surprised by the shape that was left when your partner went away?

- Who in your life do you find it easy to relate to, and why? Who do you find it difficult to relate to, and why?

- Have you ever had a relationship with someone which changed your life? What happened? In what way did the relationship change you?

- Have you ever had someone in your life go away? What happened? How did you feel?

- Have you ever had to go away from someone? What happened? Was it easy or difficult?

- Name three things that are difficult about relating to other people. Name three things that are wonderful about relating to other people.

Variations:

Before creating a relationship with one of the shapes, the mover could change one thing about the shape. For example, the mover might move the other person's arm to a different position before creating a relationship to that person. This could lead to a discussion about our desire to change the people we relate to.

Extended Activities:

Ask students to write a short essay describing a relationship that changed their life. This could be a relationship to a family member, teacher or friend. Encourage students to describe the changes in themselves that they noticed as a result of the relationship.

Lesson 18: Making an Impact

Type of Movement Activity:
Group Shapes

Related Movement Concepts:
Shapes (straight, curved, angular, twisted)
Relationships (near, far, over, under, around, through)
Body Parts (head, arms, legs, etc.)

Materials / Preparation:
None

Musical Suggestions:
No music required

Space Required:
In a regular classroom, have half of the students create the chain of shapes across the front of the room while the rest of the class watches, then switch roles. This activity could also be done by the entire class in a large, open space.

Time Required:
Approximately 10 minutes

Introduction:

Do you believe that your actions make a difference in the world? Although it's sometimes difficult to feel that the things we do really matter to anyone outside of ourselves, each one of our actions actually has a powerful effect on the people around us.

Lesson:

We're going to create a chain of shapes that stretches across the room. We'll start by having one person make an interesting shape with their body right against this wall. The next person will make a new shape that connects to the first one. They might connect to the first shape using their hands, their head, a foot, a hip or any other body part they choose. We'll keep adding shapes to the chain until there is a line of connected shapes reaching to the opposite wall of the room.

(Choose one student to begin the shape chain, and continue adding students until a line of connected shapes has been created.)

When I say "go," the first person in line will change their shape. They might suddenly become bigger or smaller, higher or lower. They might change the position of their whole body, or just one body part.

The second person in line will let the first person's movement impact them, and cause a change in their shape. Maybe the first person's change will cause them to sink or twist or go off balance. Let the original change affect each person, all the way down the line.

(Allow the group to complete this sequence. The idea is not for the students to think of ways to change their shapes, but to actually be impacted by the change in the person next to them.)

Let's try that again beginning with a change at the other end of the line.

What will happen if we start the change in the middle?

Let's try it one last time, starting with a very small, almost invisible change.

(Repeat the activity with the other half of the class, if applicable, then ask students to be seated for discussion.)

Questions for Discussion:

- How many people did the original change affect?

- If you were one of the people who started a sequence of changes, how did that feel?

- Was it possible not to be impacted by the changes around you? What would you have to do in order not to be impacted?

- How many people were impacted when the initial change was very small?

- Have you ever taken an action that changed the lives of people around you? What happened? How did it feel?

- Has your life ever been changed as the result of an action taken by someone else?

- Is it possible to take an action that does not impact the people around you?

Variations:

Instead of doing this activity in a line, it could be done with a circle of shapes, or a group of shapes that are randomly intertwined.

Try letting students randomly initiate changes at any time. In this variation there could be more than one sequence of changes taking place simultaneously.

Extended Activities:

Ask students to create a list of the ways in which they make an impact. They might begin by thinking about how they impact their families and friends, and expand to realizing ways in which they impact their school and community.

Guide the class as a whole in thinking of a way that they'd like to impact their school, community, city, country or world. Help them design and implement a project to make that vision a reality.

Section I: Trust

The deepest, most satisfying interpersonal relationships are based on mutual trust. When we trust another person we have the safety to express ourselves fully and honestly and to take risks. There is great freedom in knowing that someone will be there for us, no matter what.

The two main ingredients of trust are empathy and consistency. Through empathy we intuit how another person might feel as a result of our behavior, and therefore refrain from behaving in ways that are potentially hurtful. Through consistency in our presence and our actions we let others know that we can be counted on.

The lessons in this section will guide students in experiencing, through movement, how it feels to trust and be trusted, and what is required for the inspiration of trust.

Lesson 19: Empathy

Type of Movement Activity:
Partner Shapes

Related Movement Concepts:
Shapes (straight, curved, angular, twisted)
Body Parts (head, arms, legs, back, etc.)

Materials / Preparation:
CD player or tape deck (optional)

Musical Suggestions:
Gentle, relaxing music such as any selection from
Seagulls by Hap Palmer (see Discography)

This lesson may also be presented without music.

Space Required:
This lesson does not require traveling through space and could easily be presented in the regular classroom.

Time Required:
Approximately 10 minutes

Introduction:

What does it mean to trust someone? When you feel trust in someone you know they wouldn't intentionally hurt you or allow you to be hurt. When you trust someone it is easy to be honest and be yourself because you know you won't be judged. You trust another person when you know that they understand and care about how you feel. Being able to imagine how another person feels is called empathy.

Lesson:

(Ask one student to demonstrate the following activity with you.)

We're going to play a game called "Sculptor and Clay." Let me show you how it works. I'm the sculptor — someone who creates statues — and this (*indicate student*) is my lump of clay. I have two jobs: one job is to move my partner's body parts into different positions to create an interesting statue. My other job is to touch my partner in such a way that she (or he) trusts me not to hurt her. In order to do that I have to imagine how my partner feels as

I move each body part. I will want to move her arms, head, legs and torso gently, the same way that I would want her to move mine. I'll imagine how she feels, and try not to move any of her body parts in a way that is uncomfortable. When I'm finished creating my statue I'll copy her shape. Then we'll switch roles so she has a turn to be the sculptor.

(Demonstrate sculpting a student gently and carefully into a shape, then copying the shape you have created. Ask students to find partners, and choose who will be the sculptor first. Turn on music and allow the sculptors to create their statues. As the students work, remind them that their job is to have their partner trust them. Once each sculptor has created and copied their statue, the pair can switch roles. Turn music off when both students in each pair have finished their turn.)

Now that each of you has had a turn to be both the sculptor and the clay, we'll do the activity again. This time, though, the person who is the clay will keep their eyes closed. Notice if you trust your partner enough to allow him or her to mold you into a statue without peeking. When the sculptor is finished you may open your eyes. The sculptor will copy the shape, then you may switch roles.

(Turn on music and allow students to repeat the activity. When both partners in each group have had a turn to be both the sculptor and the clay, turn music off and ask students to be seated for discussion.)

Sculptor and clay

Questions for Discussion:

• When you were the clay did you trust your partner to move you gently? Why or why not?

• Did you feel more trustful when your eyes were open or when they were closed. Why?

• When you were the sculptor, did you feel successful in getting your partner's trust? What did you need to do to make that happen?

• As the sculptor, what were some things you had to be aware of in order to move your partner's body carefully?

• Is there anyone in your life that you completely trust? Who, and why?

• What might cause you to lose trust in someone?

• Do you feel that you are trustworthy; that people can trust you? What do you do to gain the trust of others?

Variations:

Instead of discussing the preceding questions with the entire class, write them on the board or copy them on paper and have the "Sculptor and Clay" partners discuss them with each other.

Extended Activities:

Ask students to find an example in a book, movie or television show of a situation where trust is established between two people, or a situation in which trust is broken. Ask individual students to share their examples with the class.

Lesson 20: Consistency

Type of Movement Activity:
Group Improvisational Exploration

Related Movement Concepts:
Relationship (near, far, over, under, around, through)
Weight (strong, light)

Materials / Preparation:
None

Musical Suggestions:
No music required

Space Required:
This lesson requires enough space for six to eight students to stand in a close circle. It could be presented in the regular classroom with an area cleared for the circle. It is advisable to present this lesson as a demonstration with a small group of students.

Time Required:
Approximately 10 minutes

Introduction:

One of the things that helps create trust is consistency. You are more likely to trust someone if their actions are predictable rather than constantly surprising. A trustworthy person is consistently there when they say they will be.

Lesson:

(Ask a group of six to eight students to form a tight circle with one student standing in the center. Ask the person in the center to close his or her eyes.)

We're going to do something that will require the person in the middle of the circle to have a lot of trust. Everyone on the edge of the circle please reach your arms in front of you, and stand close enough together that you can touch the center person lightly. He or she will begin to lean a little bit in any direction. If he leans toward you, support his weight with your arms, then push him back upright. Then he'll lean in a new direction. As he falls, someone will always be there to catch him and stand him back up.

(Allow students to experiment with this activity for one to two minutes. Give several students a turn to experience being in the center of the circle. If the group is working well together you may choose to have them widen the circle a bit so the person actually "falls" for a second before being caught. NOTE: This activity requires a great deal of trust and should only be attempted with students who are mature enough to understand the consequences of actually letting someone fall. You may want to do this activity on a gym mat to ensure safety.)

Questions for Discussion:

• How did it feel to be the person in the center of the circle? Did you feel afraid? Safe?

• Did you feel most trustful at first, or after you had fallen and been caught several times? Why?

• How did it feel to have the responsibility of catching the center person when they fell toward you?

- If you were watching this activity, what do you think caused the center person to trust those in the circle?

- How could you tell when the person in the center felt completely trusting?

- Is there anyone in your life that you can always count on to be there for you when you need them?

- Are you someone who can be counted on?

Variations:

If you feel that this activity is too advanced for your particular class, try it with the person in the center sitting and the people on the edge of the circle kneeling. The center person will be able to fall backward and sideways, but not forward.

Extended Activities:

Ask students to think of a person in their life whom they feel they can always count on, and to write that person a short letter of appreciation.

Section J: Cooperation

Once we have become aware and appreciative of the many similarities and differences among human beings, have opened avenues of communication and mutual trust and realized the impact that each person's contributions make, we are ready to embark on the journey of cooperation to reach a common goal. Cooperation involves a willingness to see beyond oneself, and to use one's strengths for the common good rather than for one's own recognition and gain.

Cooperation also requires the skills of compromise and negotiation. In working cooperatively with others it is sometimes necessary to let go of being in complete control of a project in order to accommodate another person's needs and viewpoints. We may find ourselves changing our original vision in order to allow for an outcome in which each participant's ideas are expressed.

The highest form of cooperation is creative collaboration, in which the end product is an integration of the diverse ideas, points of view and expressive values of the creators.

In the lessons in this section, students will experience, through movement, the skills required and the satisfaction gained in working cooperatively with others.

Lesson 21: Movement Machine

Type of Movement Activity:
Group Improvisational Exploration

Related Movement Concepts:
Place (self space, general space)
Body Parts (head, arms, legs, feet, etc.)
Relationship (near, far, over, under around, through)

Materials / Preparation:
None

Musical Suggestions:
Chappelle, Eric, "Add On Machine," *Music for Creative Dance: Contrast and Continuum, Volume I* (see Discography)

This lesson may also be presented without music.

Space Required:
This lesson requires enough space for half of the class to stand close together executing minimal movement without traveling. It could also be successfully done by a smaller group (eight to twelve students) in a cleared area of the regular classroom.

Time Required:
Approximately 10 minutes

Introduction:

I'm sure you've all heard the word "cooperation" and you've probably been asked to "cooperate" many times. But what does cooperation actually mean? It means working together with another person — or with a group of people — to reach a common goal. It's a bit like being part of a machine; helping that machine to work productively and efficiently.

Lesson:

(Divide the class in half or choose a group of eight to twelve students.)

These students are going to create a "movement machine." I will call the name of one person to begin the machine. That person will stand in one place and do a repetitive, machine-like movement. They might move an arm forward and back, or twist their body from side to side. The movement should be very simple; something that can be repeated over and over.

(Turn on music. Choose one student to come to the center of the space to begin a repetitive movement. Guide them in creating a movement if necessary.)

If I were the next person to add on to this machine I would come very close to the first person and create a repetitive movement that fits with his (or hers). It should look like I'm moving him, or he's moving me.

(Demonstrate a possible addition to the first person's movement. For example, if the first person is repeatedly moving an arm forward and pulling it back, you might move your head in sync with her arm as if your head is making her arm move.)

Now that you have the idea, who would like to come up and add on to the first person's movement?

(Allow students to add on to the machine one by one. They may add themselves to

any part of the machine, and may even do movements on different levels. When all students in the group have become part of the machine, allow the group's movement to continue for ten to twenty seconds, then turn off music. Repeat the activity with the other half of the class or a new small group. When all students have had a chance to participate in a machine, ask them to be seated for discussion.)

Movement machine

Questions for Discussion:

• Can you imagine what kind of machine you were part of or what that machine might have been making? What part did you play in making the machine work?

• How did it feel to be a part of a machine? Did you feel that you were important? Unimportant?

• Who do you think was the most important person in the machine?

• Could the machine have functioned as well if any of its parts had been missing?

• When it was your turn to add on to the machine, how did you decide where to fit in and what movement to do?

• What are some situations in life where each person must do their part to help the whole group function effectively?

• What did you learn from your experience of being part of a movement machine that might help you in a situation in which you need to cooperate with others?

• What would happen if one part of the movement machine stopped working? How is this similar to what happens when one person in a group doesn't cooperate?

Variations:

Ask each student to make a repetitive sound to go along with their movement. The combined rhythms of the sounds add another layer of complexity to the machine.

Instead of doing this activity as an improvisation, print the names of common machines (i.e.: washing machine, CD player, toaster) on cards. Give groups of four to eight students a card and ask them to illustrate, through movement, how that machine works.

Extended Activities:

Work with the class to design a project they are motivated to complete. Guide them in organizing which part of the project each person or small group will be responsible for. Discuss the consequences to the project if any one person neglects to carry out his or her responsibilities.

Lesson 22: Compromise

Type of Movement Activity:
Group Improvisational Exploration
Partner Choreography

Related Movement Concepts:
Locomotor and Non-Locomotor Movement (see "Partial Listing of Locomotor and Non-Locomotor Movements")

Rhythm (pulse, breath)

Materials / Preparation:
It will be helpful to have a copy of "A Partial Listing of Locomotor and Non-Locomotor Movements" posted during the lesson. It is suggested that you copy it on a large sheet of butcher paper for easy visibility.

Musical Suggestions:
Chappelle, Eric, "Weavers," *Music for Creative Dance: Contrast and Continuum, Volume II.* (See Discography.)

Any piece of music which is easily counted in eight-beat phrases may be used.

Space Required:
This lesson could be presented in the regular classroom with students creating movements that do not travel through space, but it will be most successful if presented in a large, open space such as an empty classroom, gym, lunchroom, stage or outdoor area.

Time Required:
Approximately 25 minutes

Introduction:

When two or more people are working together, it is natural for them to sometimes have conflicting ideas or opinions. In such situations it is important to have the skill of being able to compromise, or to find a middle ground between what each person wants. In a compromise there are no winners or losers, because everyone's ideas are valued.

Lesson:

I'm going to ask each of you to create a movement that you can do for eight counts. Looking at the chart I've put up might give you some ideas. You might decide to do something very simple like marching in place for eight counts, or you could create a more complex movement by putting two words together. For example, you might turn and slash for eight counts.

Take a moment to create a movement on your own. Raise your hand if you feel you need some help.

(Give students one to two minutes to create a movement. Circulate among them, giving assistance as needed.)

Would someone please raise their hand and show us their movement?

(Call on a student and allow him or her to show their movement to the class. Have everyone learn the movement, and perform it while counting to eight. Repeat this process with the second student.)

We now have two movement ideas. What if we had only one set of eight counts, and two ideas? Of course we could just do one of the two movements and forget about the other one, but instead let's think of a way we could compromise so we use both ideas in one set of eight counts. What are some ways we could do that?

(Allow students to respond. Possible solutions would be to do each movement for four counts, or to combine them into one movement which could be done for eight counts. Try both of these solutions, as well as any others that the students suggest.)

In a moment I will ask you to find a partner to work with. First, learn each other's movements. Then you and your partner will create a movement study that has four sets of eight counts:

One person's movement
The other person's movement
A compromise between the two movements
A shape

(NOTE: You may want to write this sequence on the board. It will also be helpful here to play the musical selection you plan to use and have the students count it aloud with you in "eights."

Have students find a partner, and allow them five to seven minutes to complete the above task. Circulate among the students giving guidance as necessary. When all the pairs have finished creating their studies, allow as many pairs as time permits to perform their studies for the class to music. Ask students to be seated for discussion.)

Questions for Discussion:

• What was it like to compromise with your partner? Did you find it easy or difficult? Why?

• In watching the other studies, were you ever surprised by the result of compromising between the two movements? Give an example.

• When in your life have you had to make a compromise? What happened? How did it feel?

• Have you ever been in a situation where you or someone else refused to compromise? What was the result?

• What do you have to give up in order to compromise?

• What is it possible to gain by compromising?

• Is it always right to compromise, or are there situations in which it's best not to make a compromise. What might some of those situations be?

Variations:

More experienced groups might take the structure of the four sets of eight counts and put the sets in their own preferred order, for example:

One person's movement
A compromise between the two movements
A shape
The other person's movement

Extended Activities:

Use this lesson as a springboard for discussing the use of compromise to resolve conflicts on the playground and in the classroom. Encourage students to experiment with making compromises at home.

Lesson 23: Collaboration

Type of Movement Activity:
Small Group Choreography

Musical Suggestions:
Any selection from Discography

Related Movement Concepts:
Relationships (near, far, over, under, around, through, together, apart)

Space Required:
This lesson requires adequate space for groups of five or six students to work simultaneously in creating choreography. It would be optimal to present this lesson in a large, open space, but also possible to present it in a regular classroom with students working on their dances in several areas of the room, or in other areas of the school building if feasible.

Materials / Preparation:
It will be very helpful to post a list of the Movement Concepts (see Movement Concepts chart, page 6), as well as a copy of "A Partial Listing of Locomotor and Non-Locomotor Movements" for students to refer to in creating their dances.

Time Required:
Approximately 30 minutes

Introduction:

One of the most complex and rewarding ways of cooperating with other people is called collaboration. In collaboration, everyone involved contributes their ideas to the finished product. No one person makes decisions, and conflicts are solved through compromise.

Lesson:

In a moment I'll divide you into groups, and you'll collaborate with your group to create a dance. The dance you create will be in an ABA form, which means that the middle section will be different from the beginning and ending sections. I'd like you to use the words "together-apart-together" as your ABA pattern. This means that in the beginning section of your dance you'll begin in a shape, then dance together. That could mean moving close together, moving over and under each other, moving in a circle or in a line together. You might all be doing the same movement or very different movements. The important thing is that you're somehow moving together.

In the middle section of your dance you'll move apart from each other. You could stretch apart slowly or burst apart quickly, you could change levels as you move apart. You'll decide with your group what kind of movement you want to do when you're dancing far apart from each other.

In the final section of your dance you will come back together. Again, you may do this in any way your group decides. You could dance together the same way you did in the first section, or in a different way. Be sure to end your dance in a shape.

The most important thing to remember as you create these dances is that every single person in your group needs to contribute at least one idea that we see when you perform the dance. If you disagree about what to do, you'll need to figure out a way to compromise. The way you work together to create your dance is more important than what the finished product will look like.

(Divide students into groups of five or six. Allow the groups twelve to fifteen minutes to create their dances. Circulate among the groups, providing assistance as needed. Once the dances have been choreographed, encourage the groups to practice them once or twice so they will be able to remember the movements.)

When all groups have finished creating their dances allow each group to perform in front of the class with music. After each performance, ask the performers to share which part of the dance each of them contributed. When all groups have had a chance to perform, discuss the following questions:

Questions for Discussion:

- How successful do you feel your group was in working collaboratively? Why or why not?

- Did every member of your group contribute at least one idea to the dance?

- Were there any conflicting ideas in your group? How did you resolve the conflict?

- Were the members of your group able to share leadership, or did you find one person in your group taking on the role of the leader? What do you think caused that to happen? *(NOTE: In discussing this it is best to refrain from pointing out particular students who were "bossy." It is not wrong to assume leadership in a group, just something for the students to notice.)*

- Did you find yourself making any compromises in order to make sure that each member of your group was able to contribute an idea to the dance?

- What are some of the challenges of collaborating with others?

- What are some of the rewards of collaborating with others?

Variations:

Instead of creating an ABA dance about the concept of Relationships, you could assign students an ABA structure using any of the other Movement Concepts, for example: Levels (low-high-low), Speed (slow-fast-slow), or Energy (smooth-sharp-smooth). (See Movement Concepts chart preceding Chapter 2.)

Extended Activities:

Ask small groups of students to write a short story collaboratively. As with the preceding movement activity, emphasize the importance of each person in a group contributing at least one idea. The finished stories could be shared verbally, spoken on tape or written on a computer.

Collaboration

Creating choreography

Section K: Leadership

To lead others effectively requires energy, focus and a clear sense of purpose. The best leaders are confident in who they are as individuals, and are committed to a goal outside of themselves. They are willing to forge ahead into the unknown, sure of the trust placed in them by those who follow. Leadership does not entail being bossy or superior; rather it expresses a willingness to be a respectful guide for others.

The lessons in this section will guide students in exploring, through movement, the qualities that comprise effective leadership.

Lesson 24:
Leading and Sharing Leadership

Type of Movement Activity:
Partner Improvisational Exploration

Related Movement Concepts:
Place (self space, general space)
Body Parts (head, elbows, feet, arms, etc.)

Materials / Preparation:
CD player or tape deck

Musical Suggestions:
Chappelle, Eric, "Adagio for Two Violins," *Music for Creative Dance: Contrast and*

Continuum: Volume I (see Discography). Any slow-paced, relaxing selection

Space Required:
This lesson does not require traveling through space and could easily be presented in the regular classroom.

Time Required:
Approximately 15 minutes

Introduction:

There may be many times in your lives when you will be called upon to be a leader. You may be a leader in your career, in politics, in your family or community. You may be a leader on your own or share leadership with others. Being a leader doesn't mean being bossy or overpowering others, rather it means to have the ability to bring out the best in other people.

Lesson:

(Choose one student to come to the front of the room to demonstrate the following procedure with you.)

We're going to do a movement activity today called "mirroring." In mirroring you will stand facing your partner. The person who is the leader will begin to move in self space; without traveling. They might stretch, curl, twist, swing, move one body part or several body parts. The other person's job is to try to move along with the leader and copy what they are doing as accurately as possible. Try to follow the leader so closely that someone watching wouldn't be able to tell who is the leader and who is the follower. When I turn off the music you will freeze; then the other person will have a turn to be the leader.

Mirroring

(Demonstrate the preceding activity with a student, then divide students into pairs. Have the pairs choose who will be the leader and who will be the follower. Turn on music and allow students to explore mirroring for one to two minutes, then turn off music. Repeat the process with reversed roles, so that each member of a pair has a turn to be the leader.)

We're going to repeat this once more, but this time no one person will be the leader; you will share leadership. Sometimes one person will begin a movement and the other partner will follow, at other times the roles will be reversed. Sometimes it may even feel as if you're both leaders at the same time. See if you can communicate with your partner about who is leading and who is following without having to speak. A person watching should simply see two people doing the same thing at the same time, without being aware of one person being the leader or follower.

(Turn on music and allow pairs to explore mirroring with shared leadership for one to two minutes. Turn music off, and ask students to be seated for discussion.)

Questions for Discussion:

- When you were the leader, what did you need to do in order for your partner to be able to follow you?

- How did it feel to be the leader? Was it exciting? Uncomfortable?

- As a follower, what kinds of movements were easiest for you to copy accurately? What were some things your leader did to help you follow?

- Did you most enjoy being a leader or a follower? Why?

- Did you feel you were successful in sharing leadership with your partner? Why or why not?

- When in your life have you been a leader? Were you successful at leading others? What did you do in order to be successful?

- When in your life have you followed the leadership of another? Was that person an effective leader? Why or why not?

- In what situations might it be important to share leadership?

- Name five qualities that you believe an effective leader needs to have.

- If you were teaching two people to share leadership, what would be the most important information to give them?

- Is it better to be a leader than a follower?

Variations:

To do this activity in groups rather than in pairs, have a group of students stand in a circle with one student leading, then with all the students in the circle sharing leadership.

Extended Activities:

Ask students to choose a person, either living or dead, whom they consider to be or have been an effective leader. Examples might be: Martin Luther King, Jr., Mahatma Gandhi, a current political leader. Have the students research the leader they have chosen and make a list of the qualities that contributed to his or her ability to lead.

Lesson 25: Changing Leadership

Type of Movement Activity:
Small Group Improvisational Exploration

Related Movement Concepts:
Relationship (near, far, over, under, around, through)
Pathways (straight, curved, zig-zag)

Materials / Preparation:
None

Musical Suggestions:
Any selection from Discography

Space Required:
This lesson will be most effectively presented in a large, open space such as an empty classroom, gym, lunchroom, stage or outdoor area.

Time Required:
Approximately 15 minutes

Introduction:

The world is always in need of leaders, and leadership is always changing. Sometimes those who have been leading need to step down and allow others to take over. At other times people who have been followers are called upon to assume leadership. Leadership may change gradually or suddenly, predictably or unexpectedly.

Lesson:

(Divide students into groups of four. Compensate for any extra students by forming trios. Temporarily take the place of a student in one of the groups to demonstrate the following sequence of directions:)

Please organize your groups into a diamond formation with everyone in the group facing in the same direction. The person at the head of the diamond will be the leader first. *(NOTE: In the case of a trio the group would form a triangle with the person at the head of the triangle being the leader.)* When the music starts, the leader will begin leading the group through general space. They could move slowly or quickly, on different levels, in straight, curved or ziz-zag pathways. The rest of the group must follow the leader and copy his or her movements, staying in the diamond (or triangle) formation.

When the leader is ready to switch leadership he or she will turn to face another person in the group. Everyone in the group will turn to face the new direction, and the person now at the front of the diamond or triangle will be the new leader. Each person may choose to be a leader for a long or short period of time, but make sure everyone in your group has at least one turn to be the leader.

(It will be helpful to have the groups practice changing their facing to switch leadership, as described above. When all groups seem comfortable with this, turn music on and allow students to explore leading, following and changing leadership for two to three minutes. Call out suggestions as they move, such as "Have you tried leading your group slowly... quickly? Have you tried skipping...jumping...marching? Try leading your group in a curved pathway or a zig-zag pathway." After two to three minutes, turn music off and ask students to be seated for discussion.)

Questions for Discussion:

- How did it feel to be a leader when you couldn't see the people following you?

- How did you decide when it was time to pass the leadership to someone else? What did you do to make the change as smooth as possible?

- How did it feel to go from being a leader to following someone else's lead?

- How did you feel when the leadership of the group was passed to you? Were you ready to take over right away, or did you feel a moment of hesitation?

- As a follower, how did it feel to follow several different leaders? Were there differences in the ways that different people led the group? If so, what were they?

- In what situations might it be important to pass on leadership to another person? What could be done to make the change in leadership happen smoothly?

- In life, what could you do to prepare yourself to assume leadership if it were passed on to you?

Variations:

With an experienced group, you may choose to ask the leaders to add repetitive vocal sounds to their movements, which would be copied by the followers.

Extended Activities:

Have students interview a teacher, family member or adult acquaintance about a time they either assumed or stepped down from a leadership position and how they prepared for the change in leadership.

Discography

The following are musical selections that can be used as background music for most of the lessons in this book. You may use one of the specific selections listed or substitute a favorite of your own. There is a separate listing of recordings that were created especially for use in teaching Creative Dance.

Day Parts, *Sunday Morning Coffee* (any selection), American Gramaphone Records, AGCD100.

Dead Can Dance, "Bird," *A Passage in Time*, Ryko, RCD 20215.

Deuter, *Call of the Unknown* (any selection), Celestial Harmonies, LC 2099.

Dietrichson, Tor, *Global Village* (any selection), Global Pacific Records, WK 40728.

Enya, "Caribbean Blue," *Shepherd Moons*, Reprise Records 4-26775.

Haun, Steve, *Inside the Sky* (any selection), Silver Wave Records SR-504.

Jarre, Jean Michel, *The Essential Jarre* (any selection), PRO L.

Jarre, Jean Michel, *Oxygene* (any selection), Polydor, PD-1-6112.

Jones, Peter and Podlesny, Joe, *The Fifth Movement* (any selection), Four Zoa Music.

Lynch, Ray, *Deep Breakfast* (any selection), RLLP-102.

Nakai, R. Carlos, *Earth Spirit* (any selection), Canyon Records, CR-612 Volume 4.

Palmer, Hap, *Seagulls* (any selection), Educational Activities, Inc., CD 584.

Penguin Café Orchestra, *Broadcasting From Home* (any selection), Editions EG, EGEDC 38.

Roth, Gabrielle and the Mirrors, *Bones* (any selection), Raven Recording.

Roth, Gabrielle and the Mirrors, *Totem* (any selection), Raven Recording LC5565.

Satie, Eric, "Gymnopedies," *Windham Hill Sampler '81*, WH1015.

Shadowfax, *Dreams of Children* (any selection), WH-1038.

Tjapukai Dancers, "Kakadu," *Proud to be Aborigine*, Jarra Hill Records, CDJHR2012.

Vollenweider, Andreas, *White Winds* (any selection), CBS FMT 39963.

Music for Creative Dance

Chappelle, Eric, *Music for Creative Dance: Contrast and Continuum, Volumes I and II* (all selections), Ravenna Ventures, Inc., RVCD 9301 and 9401.

(NOTE: The two CD's listed above contain many selections with pauses and alternating phrases, and are excellent for use in exploring the Movement Concepts. Each CD comes with a booklet of Creative Dance teaching ideas.)

Barlin, Anne, "Freeze and Move," *Hello Toes: Movement Games for Children*, Princeton Book Company. (Short selections of rhythms from different cultures.)

Pica, Rae "Robots and Astronauts," *Let's Move and Learn*. (Music with alternating free flow and bound flow sections.)

Weikart, Phyllis and Gemini, *Rhythmically Movin' Series*, High Scope Press, ISBN 0-929816-13-7. (folk dances)

For information on ordering Eric Chappelle's *Music for Creative Dance: Contrast and Continuum, Volumes I and II* write or call:

Ravenna Ventures, Inc.
4756 University Village Pl. NE. #117
Seattle, WA 98105
528-7556

Bibliography

BOOKS AND ARTICLES ON EDUCATION AND INTERPERSONAL AWARENESS

Dickinson, Dee. 1997. "Learning Through the Arts." Seattle, WA: New Horizons for Learning: http://www.newhorizons.org.

Eyre, Linda and Richard. 1993. *Teaching Your Children Values*. New York: Simon and Schuster.

Fletcher, Ruth. 1986. *Teaching Peace*. San Francisco: Harper and Row.

Gardner, Howard. 1983. *Frames of Mind*. New York: Basic Books, Inc.

Gardner, Howard. 1991. *The Unschooled Mind*. New York: Basic Books, Inc.

MacKenzie, Robert J., Ed.D. 1996. *Setting Limits in the Classroom*. California: Prima Publishing.

BOOKS ON MOVEMENT AND THE BRAIN

Ayres, Jean A., Ph.D. 1972. *Sensory Integration and Learning Disorders*. Western Psychological Services.

Delacato, Carl H. 1977. *A New Start for the Child with Reading Problems*. New York: Macmillian.

Lewinn, Dr. Edward D. 1977. *Human Neurological Organization*. Springfield, IL: Charles C. Thomas Publishers.

FOR FURTHER INFORMATION ON MOVEMENT AND THE BRAIN, WRITE TO:

Bette Lamont, Director
Developmental Movement Center
10303 Meridian Ave. N. Suite 201
PO Box 75681
Seattle, WA 98125

BOOKS ON THE WORK OF RUDOLPH VON LABAN

Bartenieff, Irmgaard with Lewis, Dori. 1980. *Body Movement: Coping With the Environment*. New York: Gordon and Breach Science Publishers.

Dell, Cecily. 1970. *A Primer for Movement Description*. New York: Center for Movement Research and Analysis Dance Notation Bureau, Inc.

Laban, Rudolph. 1971. *The Mastery of Movement: Third Edition*. Boston: Plays, Inc.

Laban, Rudolph von. 1963. *Modern Educational Dance*. Second Edition. London: MacDonald and Evans.

FOR FURTHER INFORMATION ON THE WORK OF RUDOLPH VON LABAN, WRITE OR CALL:

Laban-Bartenieff Institute for Movement Studies
11 East 4th Street 3rd Floor
New York, NY 10003
(212) 477-4299

BOOKS ON TEACHING CREATIVE MOVEMENT AND DANCE

Gilbert, Anne Green. 1992. *Creative Dance for All Ages*. Reston, VA: American Alliance for Health, Physical Education, Recreation and Dance.

Gilbert, Anne Green. 1977. *Teaching the Three R's Through Movement Experiences*. Minneapolis, MN.: Burgess Publishing Company.

Joyce, Mary. 1994. *First Steps in Teaching Creative Dance to Children*. Third Edition. Mountain View, CA: Mayfield Publishing Company.

Landalf, Helen and Gerke, Pamela. 1996. *Movement Stories for Young Children Ages 3-6*. Lyme, NH: Smith and Kraus, Inc.

Landalf, Helen. 1997. *Moving the Earth: Teaching Earth Science Through Movement in Grades 3-6*. Lyme, NH: Smith and Kraus, Inc.

Weikart, Phyllis. 1983. *Teaching Movement and Dance*. Ypsilanti, MI: High/Scope Press.

FOR FURTHER INFORMATION ON DANCE EDUCATION WRITE:

National Dance Association
American Alliance for Health, Physical Education, Recreation and Dance
1900 Association Drive
Reston, VA 22091
476-3436

Sample
Creative Dance Lesson #1

Movement Concept: Place (Self Space, General Space)
Length of Lesson: 45 minutes

Warm-up:

Have students mirror (copy) your self space (stationary) movements. Do slow, gentle movements such as stretching, slow twisting and swaying. Alternate this with having the students move freely through general space. Guide them by suggesting different movements they might try: skipping, turning, sliding, shaking. If you are uncomfortable leading this warm-up, ask a student to be the leader, or divide the students into pairs and have them mirror a partner.

Musical Suggestions: Chappelle, Eric "All and One," *Music for Creative Dance: Contrast and Continuum, Volume I.*

Concept Introduction:

Introduce students to the concept of Place by having them move in one spot as they say "Self space," and travel through the room as they say "General Space."

Concept Exploration:

Call out a non-locomotor word from the "Partial Listing of Locomotor and Non-Locomotor Movements" preceding Chapter 2. Students will explore this word in self space. Next, call out the same non-locomotor word, but add a word from the list of locomotor movements. The students will travel through general space combining the two words. For example, the non-locomotor word might be

"float," which the students would explore in self space. If the locomotor word "skip" were added, students would then do a floating skip through general space. Continue with additional word pairs.

Musical Suggestion: Chappelle, Eric, "Potpourri," *Music for Creative Dance: Contrast and Continuum, Volume I or II.*

Skill Development:

Choose two non-locomotor words and three locomotor words from the "Partial Listing of Locomotor and Non-Locomotor Movements" preceding Chapter 2, and write each of the five words on a separate 3x5 card. Have students help you put the cards in any order they choose, then have them perform the sequence of words. An example of such a sequence might be: "Roll...stretch...hop... twist...slide." You could have them do the sequence to counts (eight counts for each word, for example) or allow them to create their own timing.

Musical Suggestions: Chappelle, Eric, "Weavers," *Music for Creative Dance: Contrast and Continuum, Volume II.*

Place small traffic cones or milk cartons in a scattered formation on the floor. Students will leap over the objects. When the music pauses, students will stand next to one of the objects and move (stretch, twist, swing, float, etc.) in self space. Next, take away the milk cartons or cones and allow the students to leap over imaginary objects, stopping to dance in self space whenever the music pauses.

Musical Suggestions: Chappelle, Eric, "Chirpa Chirpa," *Music for Creative Dance: Contrast and Continuum, Volume I.*

Improvisation:

Divide students into pairs and designate one student in each pair to be the leader. The leader moves freely through general space with their partner following them and copying their movements. When the music pauses, the pair makes a shape together in self space. On the next musical phrase the second student is the leader.

Musical Suggestion: Chappelle, Eric, "Pathway Puzzle," *Music for Creative Dance: Contrast and Continuum: Volume II.*

Sample
Creative Dance Lesson #2

Movement Concept: Relationships (near, far, over, under, around, through, etc.)
Length of Lesson: 50 minutes

Warm-up:

Provide each student with a chiffon scarf. Call out a relationship word and allow students to freely explore that word with their scarf. For example if you say the word "over" students could explore leaping and jumping over their scarf, tossing the scarf over their heads or dancing while holding the scarf over their bodies. After a minute or two move on to another relationship word. If you do not have scarves available, this activity can also be done with crepe paper streamers.

Musical Suggestion: Chappelle, Eric "Ski Reel," *Music for Creative Dance: Contrast and Continuum, Volume II.*

Concept Introduction:

Introduce students to the concept of Relationships by having them try various relationships between their own body parts as they say the words "over" (perhaps holding hands overhead), "under" (perhaps placing a hand under a foot), "around" (putting arms around a body part) and "through" (creating an opening with an arm or leg and putting another body part through the opening.)

Concept Exploration:

Divide the class in half and instruct half of the students to find an empty spot to stand and make frozen shapes with their bodies. When the music begins, the remaining students will move over, under, around and through the shapes. When the music stops the dancers will choose one shape to create a relationship with. For example, if the original shape was wide and open, the dancer might make a smaller shape to fit inside. When the music begins again the original shapes become the dancers and the original dancers make new shapes.

Musical Suggestion: Chappelle, Eric, "Pastorale," *Music for Creative Dance: Contrast and Continuum: Volume II.*

Skill Development:

Teach students a circle folk dance such as the Israeli dance "Mayim." Emphasize the relationships in the dance: moving near and far from one another, circling around a point in space, etc. Instructions for many folk dances can be found in Phyllis Weikart's book *Teaching Movement and Dance* (see Bibliography).

Musical Suggestion: "Mayim" (Israeli folk dance), Weikart, Phyllis and Gemeni, *Rhythmically Movin' 5.*

Choreography:

Have small groups (4-6 students) create dances in an A-B-C form where part A emphasizes body part relationships, part B emphasizes relationships to props (scarves, crepe paper streamers, etc.) and part C emphasizes relationships between dancers. Students collaboratively plan how they will show each type of relationship, and how they will transition from one section to the next. Allow students 10-15 minutes to plan and practice their dances, then give each group an opportunity to perform for their peers. Ask the audience members to give the performers positive feedback on their dance, discussing the types of relationships they saw and what made the dance interesting to watch.

Musical Suggestion: Chappelle, Eric, "Jammin' On the Porch," *Music for Creative Dance: Contrast and Continuum, Volume I.*

ABOUT THE AUTHOR

Helen Landalf is author of *The Secret Night World of Cats, Moving the Earth: Teaching Earth Science through Movement in Grades 3-6*, and co-author of *Movement Stories for Children ages 3-6* with Pamela Gerke, all published by Smith & Kraus, Inc. She has been teaching, choreographing and performing dance in the Seattle area since 1987, with an emphasis on teaching creative and modern dance to children. She is on the faculty of the Creative Dance Center in Seattle and has served as an Artist in Residence for the Montana Public Schools. She frequently presents workshops for preschool and classroom teachers on integrating dance into the basic curriculum.

ABOUT THE PHOTOGRAPHER

Thomas Christopher is a native Washingtonian who currently resides in the city of Seattle. He makes his living as a commercial photographer.